Women in the Labor Force:
A Databook

U.S. Department of Labor
Hilda L. Solis, Secretary

U.S. Bureau of Labor Statistics
Keith Hall, Commissioner

September 2009

Report 1018

Contents

Contents—Continued

Women in the Labor Force: A Databook

Introduction

The past several decades have been marked by notable changes in women's labor force activities. Women's labor force participation is significantly higher today than it was in the 1970s, particularly among women with children, and a larger share of women work full time and year round than in past decades. In addition, women have increasingly attained higher levels of education: among women aged 25 to 64 who are in the labor force, the proportion with a college degree roughly tripled from 1970 to 2008. Women's earnings as a proportion of men's earnings also have grown over time. In 1979, women working full time earned 62 percent of what men did; in 2008, women's earnings were 80 percent of men's.

This report presents historical and current labor force and earnings data for women and men from the Current Population Survey (CPS). The CPS is a national monthly survey of approximately 60,000 households conducted by the U.S. Census Bureau for the U.S. Bureau of Labor Statistics. Unless otherwise noted, data are annual averages from the CPS. Users should note that the comparisons of earnings in this report are on a broad level and do not control for many factors that can be significant in explaining earnings differences. For a detailed description of the source of the data and an explanation of concepts and definitions used, see the Technical Note at the end of this report.

Highlights

- In 2008, 59.5 percent of women were in the labor force, and this share has been relatively stable over the past several years. Women's labor force participation rate peaked at 60 percent in 1999, following several decades in which women increasingly entered the labor market. (See tables 1 and 2.)

- In 2008, the overall unemployment rate for women was 5.4 percent, but rates varied by race and Hispanic ethnicity. Asian women had the lowest rate (3.7 percent), followed by white (4.9 percent), Hispanic (7.7 percent), and black (8.9 percent) women. (See tables 1, 2, and 3.)

- From March 1975 to March 2000, the labor force participation rate of mothers with children under age 18 rose from 47 percent to a peak of 73 percent. (These data were collected in the March CPS.) By 2004, the participation rate for mothers had receded to 71 percent, where it remained through 2008. (See tables 6 and 7.)

- In general, mothers with older children (6 to 17 years of age, none younger) are more likely to participate in the labor force than mothers with younger children (under 6 years of age), and unmarried mothers have higher participation rates than married mothers. In 2008, 76 percent of unmarried mothers were in the labor force, compared with 69 percent of married mothers. (See tables 6 and 7.)

- The educational attainment of women aged 25 to 64 in the labor force rose substantially from 1970 to 2008. Thirty-six percent of these women held college degrees in 2008, compared with 11 percent in 1970. Only 7 percent of women were high school dropouts in 2008, down from 34 percent in 1970. (See table 9.)

- In 2008, women accounted for 51 percent of all persons employed in management, professional, and related occupations, somewhat more than their share of total employment (47 percent). The share of women in specific occupations within this broad category varied. For example, 8 percent of construction managers and 34 percent of lawyers were women, while 61 percent of accountants and 79 percent of social workers were women. (See table 11.)

- Employed Asian women were more likely (46 percent) to work in the higher paying management, professional, and related occupations in 2008 than were employed white (41 percent), black (31 percent), or Hispanic (24 percent) women. Meanwhile, Hispanic women (31 percent) and black women (28 percent) were more likely than white and Asian women (each 19 percent) to work in service occupations. (See table 12.)

- In 2008, women accounted for more than half of all workers within several industry sectors: financial activities, education and health services, leisure and hospitality, and other services. However, women were substantially underrepresented (relative to their share of total employment) in agriculture, mining, construction, manufacturing, and transportation and utilities. (See table 14.)

- Women who worked full time in wage and salary jobs had median usual weekly earnings of $638 in 2008. This represented 80 percent of men's median weekly earnings ($798). Earnings of Asian ($753) and white ($654) women were substantially higher than the earnings of their black ($554) and Hispanic ($501) counterparts. Women's-to-men's earnings ratios were higher among blacks (89 percent) and Hispanics (90 percent) than among whites (79 percent) and Asians (78 percent). (See table 16.)

- In 2008, female full-time wage and salary workers aged 25 and older with only a high school diploma had median usual weekly earnings of $520. This represented 79 percent of the earnings for women with an associate degree ($661), and 54 percent of those for women with a bachelor's degree or higher ($955). (See table 17.)

- In 2008, 25 percent of employed women usually worked part time—fewer than 35 hours per week. In comparison, 11 percent of employed men usually worked part time. (See table 20.)

- Women in nonagricultural industries worked an average of 36.1 hours per week in 2008. The average workweek for men in nonagricultural industries was 41.2 hours. (See table 21.)

- Of all women who worked at some point during calendar year 2007, 62 percent worked full time and year round, compared with 41 percent in 1970. During the same period, the proportion of men who worked full time and year round grew from 66 to 75 percent. (See table 22.) (These data were collected in the 1971 and 2008 Annual Social and Economic Supplement to the CPS and refer to work experience during the prior calendar year.)

- Both the wife and husband had earnings from work in 58 percent of married-couple families in 2007, up from 44 percent in 1967. Couples in which only the husband worked represented 18 percent of married-couple families in 2007, compared with 36 percent in 1967. (See table 23.) (These data were collected in the 1968 and 2008 Annual Social and Economic Supplement to the CPS and reflect earnings and work experience of the prior calendar year.)

- In 2007, working wives contributed 36 percent of their families' incomes, up by 9 percentage points from 1970, when wives' earnings accounted for 27 percent of their families' total incomes. The proportion of wives earning more than their husbands also has grown. In 1987, 18 percent of working wives whose husbands also worked earned more than their spouses; in 2007, the proportion was 26 percent. (See tables 24 and 25.) (These data were collected in the 1971, 1988, and 2008 Annual Social and Economic Supplement to the CPS and reflect earnings and work experience of the prior calendar year.)

- In 2008, approximately 1.5 million women paid at an hourly rate had earnings at or below the prevailing Federal minimum wage. This represented 4 percent of all women paid at an hourly rate. Among women 25 years and older who were paid hourly rates, 3 percent had earnings at or below the minimum wage, compared with 10 percent of women aged 16 to 24. (On July 24, 2008, the Federal minimum wage level rose from $5.85 to $6.55 an hour. Data in this report reflect the average number of workers who earned $5.85 or less from January 2008 through July 2008 and those who earned $6.55 or less from August 2008 through the end of the year.) (See table 26.)

- Among workers who were in the labor force for at least 27 weeks in 2007, women were slightly more likely than men to live in poverty—6 percent, compared with 5 percent. Black and Hispanic women who were in the labor force for 27 weeks or more were significantly more likely than their white or Asian counterparts to be among the working poor. The poverty rates for black and Hispanic working women were 12 percent and 11 percent, respectively, compared with 5 percent and 4 percent, respectively, for white and Asian women. (See table 27.) (Data are from the 2008 Annual Social and Economic Supplement to the CPS and reflect earnings and work experience of the prior calendar year.)

- Among 2008 high school graduates, young women (72 percent) were somewhat more likely than young men (66 percent) to be enrolled in college in October 2008. (See table 33.) (Data are from the October 2008 School Enrollment Supplement to the CPS.)

- In October 2008, 45 percent of women aged 16 to 24 who were enrolled in either high school or college were in the labor force. Young men of the same age group who were enrolled in school had a lower labor force participation rate (39 percent). Among those not enrolled in school, women were less likely to be in the labor force than men (74 percent, compared with 85 percent). (See table 34.) (Data are from the October 2008 School Enrollment Supplement to the CPS.)

- Among 16- to 24-year-old women who were not enrolled in school, those who did not have a high school diploma were significantly less likely to participate in the labor force than those who had a high school diploma but no additional education (50 percent, compared with 71 percent). Of those in the labor force, the high school dropouts were more likely to be unemployed than the high school graduates (25 percent, compared with 13 percent). (See table 34.) (Data are from the October 2008 School Enrollment Supplement to the CPS.)

- In May 2008, 5.6 percent of employed women held more than one job, nearly the same as the previous year. The May 2008 multiple jobholding rate for men was lower, at 4.9 percent. Multiple jobholding rates for both women and men have declined since the mid-1990s. (See table 35.) (Data were collected in the May CPS.)

- Since 1976, the percentage of working women who were self-employed has trended up (from 4.4 percent in 1976 to 5.2 percent in 2008), while the percentage of men who were self-employed has edged down (from 8.4 percent to 7.6 percent). In 2008, 38 percent of all self-employed persons were women, compared with 27 percent in 1976. (See table 36.)

- In 2008, foreign-born women were less likely than native-born women to be in the labor force (55 percent, compared with 60 percent). Of those in the labor force, native-born women were less likely to be unemployed (5.3 and 6.0 percent, respectively). Among men, the opposite was true. Foreign-born men were more likely than the native born to be in the labor force (81 percent, compared with 71 percent) and somewhat less likely to be unemployed (5.7 and 6.2 percent, respectively). (See table 37.)

- Thirteen percent of female wage and salary workers were represented by unions in 2008, compared with 15 percent of men. Union attachment for both sexes had been on a downward trend since 1983, when unions represented 18 percent of women and 28 percent of men in wage and salary jobs. Over the past 2 years, however, union representation has increased slightly among both women and men, from lows in 2006 of 12 percent and 14 percent, respectively. (See table 38.)

Table 1. Employment status of the civilian noninstitutional population by age and sex, 2008 annual averages

(Numbers in thousands)

Age	Civilian noninsti-tutional population	Civilian labor force						Not in labor force
		Total	Percent of population	Employed		Unemployed		
				Total	Percent of population	Total	Percent of labor force	
Total, both sexes								
16 years and over	233,788	154,287	66.0	145,362	62.2	8,924	5.8	79,501
16 to 19 years	17,075	6,858	40.2	5,573	32.6	1,285	18.7	10,218
16 to 17 years.........	9,133	2,552	27.9	1,989	21.8	563	22.1	6,581
18 to 19 years.........	7,942	4,306	54.2	3,584	45.1	722	16.8	3,637
20 to 24 years...........	20,409	15,174	74.4	13,629	66.8	1,545	10.2	5,234
25 to 54 years...........	125,652	104,396	83.1	99,369	79.1	5,027	4.8	21,255
25 to 34 years.........	39,993	33,332	83.3	31,383	78.5	1,949	5.8	6,661
25 to 29 years......	20,815	17,293	83.1	16,171	77.7	1,122	6.5	3,522
30 to 34 years......	19,179	16,039	83.6	15,212	79.3	827	5.2	3,139
35 to 44 years.........	41,699	35,061	84.1	33,457	80.2	1,604	4.6	6,638
35 to 39 years......	20,537	17,218	83.8	16,408	79.9	810	4.7	3,319
40 to 44 years......	21,162	17,843	84.3	17,049	80.6	795	4.5	3,318
45 to 54 years.........	43,960	36,003	81.9	34,529	78.5	1,473	4.1	7,957
45 to 49 years......	22,644	18,870	83.3	18,106	80.0	764	4.0	3,774
50 to 54 years......	21,316	17,133	80.4	16,423	77.0	710	4.1	4,183
55 to 64 years...........	33,491	21,615	64.5	20,812	62.1	803	3.7	11,876
55 to 59 years.........	18,444	13,480	73.1	12,969	70.3	511	3.8	4,964
60 to 64 years.........	15,047	8,135	54.1	7,843	52.1	292	3.6	6,912
65 years and over........	37,161	6,243	16.8	5,979	16.1	264	4.2	30,918
65 to 69 years.........	11,242	3,451	30.7	3,307	29.4	144	4.2	7,791
70 to 74 years.........	8,639	1,534	17.8	1,462	16.9	72	4.7	7,105
75 years and over....	17,281	1,258	7.3	1,211	7.0	48	3.8	16,023

Table 1. **Employment status of the civilian noninstitutional population by age and sex, 2008 annual averages—Continued**

(Numbers in thousands)

Age	Civilian noninsti-tutional population	Civilian labor force						Not in labor force
		Total	Percent of population	Employed		Unemployed		
				Total	Percent of population	Total	Percent of labor force	
Women								
16 years and over	120,675	71,767	59.5	67,876	56.2	3,891	5.4	48,908
16 to 19 years	8,415	3,385	40.2	2,837	33.7	549	16.2	5,030
16 to 17 years.........	4,508	1,314	29.2	1,063	23.6	251	19.1	3,194
18 to 19 years.........	3,907	2,071	53.0	1,774	45.4	297	14.3	1,836
20 to 24 years...........	10,160	7,109	70.0	6,484	63.8	625	8.8	3,050
25 to 54 years...........	63,574	48,195	75.8	45,965	72.3	2,229	4.6	15,379
25 to 34 years.........	19,994	15,030	75.2	14,200	71.0	830	5.5	4,964
25 to 29 years......	10,363	7,862	75.9	7,397	71.4	466	5.9	2,501
30 to 34 years......	9,631	7,168	74.4	6,803	70.6	365	5.1	2,463
35 to 44 years.........	21,132	16,089	76.1	15,360	72.7	730	4.5	5,043
35 to 39 years......	10,395	7,814	75.2	7,437	71.5	377	4.8	2,581
40 to 44 years......	10,737	8,275	77.1	7,922	73.8	353	4.3	2,462
45 to 54 years.........	22,448	17,075	76.1	16,406	73.1	669	3.9	5,372
45 to 49 years......	11,536	8,908	77.2	8,565	74.2	343	3.9	2,628
50 to 54 years......	10,912	8,167	74.8	7,841	71.9	326	4.0	2,744
55 to 64 years...........	17,367	10,270	59.1	9,893	57.0	377	3.7	7,097
55 to 59 years.........	9,515	6,445	67.7	6,199	65.2	246	3.8	3,070
60 to 64 years.........	7,852	3,825	48.7	3,694	47.0	132	3.4	4,027
65 years and over......	21,160	2,808	13.3	2,697	12.7	111	3.9	18,352
65 to 69 years.........	5,995	1,585	26.4	1,528	25.5	57	3.6	4,410
70 to 74 years.........	4,728	676	14.3	644	13.6	32	4.7	4,052
75 years and over....	10,437	547	5.2	525	5.0	22	4.0	9,890

Table 1. **Employment status of the civilian noninstitutional population by age and sex, 2008 annual averages—Continued**

(Numbers in thousands)

Age	Civilian noninsti- tutional population	Civilian labor force						Not in labor force
		Total	Percent of population	Employed		Unemployed		
				Total	Percent of population	Total	Percent of labor force	
				Men				
16 years and over	113,113	82,520	73.0	77,486	68.5	5,033	6.1	30,593
16 to 19 years	8,660	3,472	40.1	2,736	31.6	736	21.2	5,188
16 to 17 years.........	4,625	1,238	26.8	926	20.0	312	25.2	3,387
18 to 19 years.........	4,035	2,235	55.4	1,810	44.9	425	19.0	1,800
20 to 24 years............	10,249	8,065	78.7	7,145	69.7	920	11.4	2,184
25 to 54 years............	62,078	56,202	90.5	53,404	86.0	2,798	5.0	5,876
25 to 34 years.........	19,999	18,302	91.5	17,183	85.9	1,119	6.1	1,697
25 to 29 years......	10,451	9,431	90.2	8,774	84.0	657	7.0	1,020
30 to 34 years......	9,548	8,871	92.9	8,409	88.1	462	5.2	677
35 to 44 years.........	20,567	18,972	92.2	18,097	88.0	875	4.6	1,595
35 to 39 years......	10,142	9,404	92.7	8,971	88.4	433	4.6	739
40 to 44 years......	10,425	9,568	91.8	9,126	87.5	442	4.6	857
45 to 54 years.........	21,512	18,928	88.0	18,124	84.2	804	4.2	2,584
45 to 49 years......	11,108	9,962	89.7	9,541	85.9	420	4.2	1,146
50 to 54 years......	10,404	8,966	86.2	8,582	82.5	383	4.3	1,438
55 to 64 years............	16,123	11,345	70.4	10,919	67.7	425	3.8	4,779
55 to 59 years.........	8,929	7,035	78.8	6,770	75.8	265	3.8	1,894
60 to 64 years.........	7,194	4,310	59.9	4,149	57.7	160	3.7	2,885
65 years and over.......	16,002	3,436	21.5	3,282	20.5	153	4.5	12,566
65 to 69 years.........	5,246	1,866	35.6	1,779	33.9	87	4.7	3,380
70 to 74 years.........	3,912	858	21.9	818	20.9	40	4.7	3,053
75 years and over....	6,844	711	10.4	685	10.0	26	3.6	6,133

SOURCE: Current Population Survey, U.S. Department of Labor, U.S. Bureau of Labor Statistics.

Table 2. **Employment status of the civilian noninstitutional population 16 years and over by sex, 1970-2008 annual averages**

(Numbers in thousands)

Year	Civilian noninstitutional population	Civilian labor force							Not in labor force
		Total	Percent of population	Employed		Unemployed			
				Total	Percent of population	Total	Percent of labor force		
	Total, both sexes								
1970.........	137,085	82,771	60.4	78,678	57.5	4,093	4.9		54,315
1971.........	140,216	84,382	60.2	79,367	56.6	5,016	5.9		55,834
1972 [1]......	144,126	87,034	60.4	82,153	57.0	4,882	5.6		57,091
1973 [1]......	147,096	89,429	60.8	85,064	57.8	4,365	4.9		57,667
1974.........	150,120	91,949	61.3	86,794	57.8	5,156	5.6		58,171
1975.........	153,153	93,775	61.2	85,846	56.1	7,929	8.5		59,377
1976.........	156,150	96,158	61.6	88,752	56.8	7,406	7.7		59,991
1977.........	159,033	99,009	62.3	92,017	57.9	6,991	7.1		60,025
1978 [1]......	161,910	102,251	63.2	96,048	59.3	6,202	6.1		59,659
1979.........	164,863	104,962	63.7	98,824	59.9	6,137	5.8		59,900
1980.........	167,745	106,940	63.8	99,303	59.2	7,637	7.1		60,806
1981.........	170,130	108,670	63.9	100,397	59.0	8,273	7.6		61,460
1982.........	172,271	110,204	64.0	99,526	57.8	10,678	9.7		62,067
1983.........	174,215	111,550	64.0	100,834	57.9	10,717	9.6		62,665
1984.........	176,383	113,544	64.4	105,005	59.5	8,539	7.5		62,839
1985.........	178,206	115,461	64.8	107,150	60.1	8,312	7.2		62,744
1986 [1]......	180,587	117,834	65.3	109,597	60.7	8,237	7.0		62,752
1987.........	182,753	119,865	65.6	112,440	61.5	7,425	6.2		62,888
1988.........	184,613	121,669	65.9	114,968	62.3	6,701	5.5		62,944
1989.........	186,393	123,869	66.5	117,342	63.0	6,528	5.3		62,523
1990 [1]......	189,164	125,840	66.5	118,793	62.8	7,047	5.6		63,324
1991.........	190,925	126,346	66.2	117,718	61.7	8,628	6.8		64,578
1992.........	192,805	128,105	66.4	118,492	61.5	9,613	7.5		64,700
1993.........	194,838	129,200	66.3	120,259	61.7	8,940	6.9		65,638
1994 [1]......	196,814	131,056	66.6	123,060	62.5	7,996	6.1		65,758
1995.........	198,584	132,304	66.6	124,900	62.9	7,404	5.6		66,280
1996.........	200,591	133,943	66.8	126,708	63.2	7,236	5.4		66,647
1997 [1]......	203,133	136,297	67.1	129,558	63.8	6,739	4.9		66,837
1998 [1]......	205,220	137,673	67.1	131,463	64.1	6,210	4.5		67,547
1999 [1]......	207,753	139,368	67.1	133,488	64.3	5,880	4.2		68,385
2000 [1]......	212,577	142,583	67.1	136,891	64.4	5,692	4.0		69,994
2001	215,092	143,734	66.8	136,933	63.7	6,801	4.7		71,359
2002	217,570	144,863	66.6	136,485	62.7	8,378	5.8		72,707
2003 [1]......	221,168	146,510	66.2	137,736	62.3	8,774	6.0		74,658
2004 [1]......	223,357	147,401	66.0	139,252	62.3	8,149	5.5		75,956
2005.........	226,082	149,320	66.0	141,730	62.7	7,591	5.1		76,762
2006.........	228,815	151,428	66.2	144,427	63.1	7,001	4.6		77,387
2007.........	231,867	153,124	66.0	146,047	63.0	7,078	4.6		78,743
2008 [1]......	233,788	154,287	66.0	145,362	62.2	8,924	5.8		79,501

See footnote at end of table.

Table 2. **Employment status of the civilian noninstitutional population 16 years and over by sex, 1970-2008 annual averages—Continued**

(Numbers in thousands)

Year	Civilian noninsti-tutional population	Civilian labor force						Not in labor force
		Total	Percent of population	Employed		Unemployed		
				Total	Percent of population	Total	Percent of labor force	
				Women				
1970..........	72,782	31,543	43.3	29,688	40.8	1,855	5.9	41,239
1971..........	74,274	32,202	43.4	29,976	40.4	2,227	6.9	42,072
1972 [1]........	76,290	33,479	43.9	31,257	41.0	2,222	6.6	42,811
1973 [1]........	77,804	34,804	44.7	32,715	42.0	2,089	6.0	43,000
1974..........	79,312	36,211	45.7	33,769	42.6	2,441	6.7	43,101
1975..........	80,860	37,475	46.3	33,989	42.0	3,486	9.3	43,386
1976..........	82,390	38,983	47.3	35,615	43.2	3,369	8.6	43,406
1977..........	83,840	40,613	48.4	37,289	44.5	3,324	8.2	43,227
1978 [1]........	85,334	42,631	50.0	39,569	46.4	3,061	7.2	42,703
1979..........	86,843	44,235	50.9	41,217	47.5	3,018	6.8	42,608
1980..........	88,348	45,487	51.5	42,117	47.7	3,370	7.4	42,861
1981..........	89,618	46,696	52.1	43,000	48.0	3,696	7.9	42,922
1982..........	90,748	47,755	52.6	43,256	47.7	4,499	9.4	42,993
1983..........	91,684	48,503	52.9	44,047	48.0	4,457	9.2	43,181
1984..........	92,778	49,709	53.6	45,915	49.5	3,794	7.6	43,068
1985..........	93,736	51,050	54.5	47,259	50.4	3,791	7.4	42,686
1986 [1]........	94,789	52,413	55.3	48,706	51.4	3,707	7.1	42,376
1987..........	95,853	53,658	56.0	50,334	52.5	3,324	6.2	42,195
1988..........	96,756	54,742	56.6	51,696	53.4	3,046	5.6	42,014
1989..........	97,630	56,030	57.4	53,027	54.3	3,003	5.4	41,601
1990 [1]........	98,787	56,829	57.5	53,689	54.3	3,140	5.5	41,957
1991..........	99,646	57,178	57.4	53,496	53.7	3,683	6.4	42,468
1992..........	100,535	58,141	57.8	54,052	53.8	4,090	7.0	42,394
1993..........	101,506	58,795	57.9	54,910	54.1	3,885	6.6	42,711
1994 [1]........	102,460	60,239	58.8	56,610	55.3	3,629	6.0	42,221
1995..........	103,406	60,944	58.9	57,523	55.6	3,421	5.6	42,462
1996..........	104,385	61,857	59.3	58,501	56.0	3,356	5.4	42,528
1997 [1]........	105,418	63,036	59.8	59,873	56.8	3,162	5.0	42,382
1998 [1]........	106,462	63,714	59.8	60,771	57.1	2,944	4.6	42,748
1999 [1]........	108,031	64,855	60.0	62,042	57.4	2,814	4.3	43,175
2000 [1]........	110,613	66,303	59.9	63,586	57.5	2,717	4.1	44,310
2001	111,811	66,848	59.8	63,737	57.0	3,111	4.7	44,962
2002	112,985	67,363	59.6	63,582	56.3	3,781	5.6	45,621
2003 [1]........	114,733	68,272	59.5	64,404	56.1	3,868	5.7	46,461
2004 [1]........	115,647	68,421	59.2	64,728	56.0	3,694	5.4	47,225
2005..........	116,931	69,288	59.3	65,757	56.2	3,531	5.1	47,643
2006..........	118,210	70,173	59.4	66,925	56.6	3,247	4.6	48,037
2007..........	119,694	70,988	59.3	67,792	56.6	3,196	4.5	48,707
2008 [1]........	120,675	71,767	59.5	67,876	56.2	3,891	5.4	48,908

See footnote at end of table.

Table 2. **Employment status of the civilian noninstitutional population 16 years and over by sex, 1970-2008 annual averages—Continued**

(Numbers in thousands)

Year	Civilian noninsti- tutional population	Civilian labor force						Not in labor force
		Total	Percent of population	Employed		Unemployed		
				Total	Percent of population	Total	Percent of labor force	
Men								
1970.........	64,304	51,228	79.7	48,990	76.2	2,238	4.4	13,076
1971.........	65,942	52,180	79.1	49,390	74.9	2,789	5.3	13,762
1972 [1]........	67,835	53,555	78.9	50,896	75.0	2,659	5.0	14,280
1973 [1]........	69,292	54,624	78.8	52,349	75.5	2,275	4.2	14,667
1974.........	70,808	55,739	78.7	53,024	74.9	2,714	4.9	15,069
1975.........	72,291	56,299	77.9	51,857	71.7	4,442	7.9	15,993
1976.........	73,759	57,174	77.5	53,138	72.0	4,036	7.1	16,585
1977.........	75,193	58,396	77.7	54,728	72.8	3,667	6.3	16,797
1978 [1]........	76,576	59,620	77.9	56,479	73.8	3,142	5.3	16,956
1979.........	78,020	60,726	77.8	57,607	73.8	3,120	5.1	17,293
1980.........	79,398	61,453	77.4	57,186	72.0	4,267	6.9	17,945
1981.........	80,511	61,974	77.0	57,397	71.3	4,577	7.4	18,537
1982.........	81,523	62,450	76.6	56,271	69.0	6,179	9.9	19,073
1983.........	82,531	63,047	76.4	56,787	68.8	6,260	9.9	19,484
1984.........	83,605	63,835	76.4	59,091	70.7	4,744	7.4	19,771
1985.........	84,469	64,411	76.3	59,891	70.9	4,521	7.0	20,058
1986 [1]........	85,798	65,422	76.3	60,892	71.0	4,530	6.9	20,376
1987.........	86,899	66,207	76.2	62,107	71.5	4,101	6.2	20,692
1988.........	87,857	66,927	76.2	63,273	72.0	3,655	5.5	20,930
1989.........	88,762	67,840	76.4	64,315	72.5	3,525	5.2	20,923
1990 [1]........	90,377	69,011	76.4	65,104	72.0	3,906	5.7	21,367
1991.........	91,278	69,168	75.8	64,223	70.4	4,946	7.2	22,110
1992.........	92,270	69,964	75.8	64,440	69.8	5,523	7.9	22,306
1993.........	93,332	70,404	75.4	65,349	70.0	5,055	7.2	22,927
1994 [1]........	94,355	70,817	75.1	66,450	70.4	4,367	6.2	23,538
1995.........	95,178	71,360	75.0	67,377	70.8	3,983	5.6	23,818
1996.........	96,206	72,087	74.9	68,207	70.9	3,880	5.4	24,119
1997 [1]........	97,715	73,261	75.0	69,685	71.3	3,577	4.9	24,454
1998 [1]........	98,758	73,959	74.9	70,693	71.6	3,266	4.4	24,799
1999 [1]........	99,722	74,512	74.7	71,446	71.6	3,066	4.1	25,210
2000 [1]........	101,964	76,280	74.8	73,305	71.9	2,975	3.9	25,684
2001	103,282	76,886	74.4	73,196	70.9	3,690	4.8	26,396
2002	104,585	77,500	74.1	72,903	69.7	4,597	5.9	27,085
2003 [1]........	106,435	78,238	73.5	73,332	68.9	4,906	6.3	28,197
2004 [1]........	107,710	78,980	73.3	74,524	69.2	4,456	5.6	28,730
2005.........	109,151	80,033	73.3	75,973	69.6	4,059	5.1	29,119
2006.........	110,605	81,255	73.5	77,502	70.1	3,753	4.6	29,350
2007.........	112,173	82,136	73.2	78,254	69.8	3,882	4.7	30,036
2008 [1]........	113,113	82,520	73.0	77,486	68.5	5,033	6.1	30,593

[1] The comparability of historical labor force data has been affected at various times by methodological and conceptual changes in the Current Population Survey (CPS). For an explanation, see the Historical Comparability section of the Household Data technical documentation provided at **http://www.bls.gov/cps/eetech_methods.pdf**.

SOURCE: Current Population Survey, U.S. Department of Labor, U.S. Bureau of Labor Statistics.

Table 3. **Employment status by race, age, sex, and Hispanic or Latino ethnicity, 2008 annual averages**

(Numbers in thousands)

Race, age, sex, and Hispanic or Latino ethnicity	Civilian noninsti-tutional population	Civilian labor force						Not in labor force
		Total	Percent of population	Employed		Unemployed		
				Total	Percent of population	Total	Percent of labor force	
White								
Total, 16 years and over.......	189,540	125,635	66.3	119,126	62.8	6,509	5.2	63,905
16 to 19 years.................	13,084	5,644	43.1	4,697	35.9	947	16.8	7,440
20 to 24 years.................	15,914	12,142	76.3	11,055	69.5	1,087	9.0	3,773
25 to 54 years.................	100,268	83,922	83.7	80,297	80.1	3,625	4.3	16,346
55 to 64 years.................	28,109	18,464	65.7	17,829	63.4	634	3.4	9,646
65 years and over............	32,165	5,463	17.0	5,247	16.3	216	4.0	26,702
Women, 16 years and over...	96,814	57,284	59.2	54,501	56.3	2,782	4.9	39,531
16 to 19 years.................	6,414	2,776	43.3	2,377	37.1	399	14.4	3,639
20 to 24 years.................	7,842	5,616	71.6	5,197	66.3	419	7.5	2,226
25 to 54 years.................	49,954	37,866	75.8	36,291	72.6	1,575	4.2	12,088
55 to 64 years.................	14,411	8,609	59.7	8,312	57.7	298	3.5	5,802
65 years and over............	18,193	2,417	13.3	2,325	12.8	92	3.8	15,776
Men, 16 years and over.......	92,725	68,351	73.7	64,624	69.7	3,727	5.5	24,374
16 to 19 years.................	6,669	2,868	43.0	2,320	34.8	548	19.1	3,801
20 to 24 years.................	8,072	6,526	80.8	5,858	72.6	668	10.2	1,546
25 to 54 years.................	50,314	46,056	91.5	44,006	87.5	2,050	4.5	4,258
55 to 64 years.................	13,698	9,855	71.9	9,518	69.5	337	3.4	3,844
65 years and over............	13,972	3,046	21.8	2,922	20.9	124	4.1	10,926
Black or African American								
Total, 16 years and over.......	27,843	17,740	63.7	15,953	57.3	1,788	10.1	10,103
16 to 19 years.................	2,676	787	29.4	541	20.2	246	31.2	1,889
20 to 24 years.................	2,914	1,981	68.0	1,625	55.8	355	17.9	933
25 to 54 years.................	15,643	12,589	80.5	11,555	73.9	1,034	8.2	3,054
55 to 64 years.................	3,429	1,908	55.6	1,791	52.2	117	6.1	1,521
65 years and over............	3,182	476	15.0	440	13.8	36	7.5	2,706
Women, 16 years and over...	15,328	9,393	61.3	8,554	55.8	839	8.9	5,934
16 to 19 years.................	1,354	402	29.7	294	21.7	108	26.8	952
20 to 24 years.................	1,530	997	65.2	831	54.3	166	16.6	533
25 to 54 years.................	8,597	6,688	77.8	6,193	72.0	495	7.4	1,909
55 to 64 years.................	1,910	1,056	55.3	1,000	52.3	56	5.3	854
65 years and over............	1,937	251	13.0	236	12.2	15	5.8	1,686
Men, 16 years and over.......	12,516	8,347	66.7	7,398	59.1	949	11.4	4,169
16 to 19 years.................	1,322	385	29.1	247	18.7	138	35.9	937
20 to 24 years.................	1,384	984	71.1	794	57.4	190	19.3	400
25 to 54 years.................	7,046	5,901	83.7	5,362	76.1	539	9.1	1,146
55 to 64 years.................	1,519	852	56.1	792	52.1	61	7.1	666
65 years and over............	1,245	225	18.1	204	16.4	21	9.5	1,020

10

Table 3. **Employment status by race, age, sex, and Hispanic or Latino ethnicity, 2008 annual averages—Continued**

(Numbers in thousands)

Race, age, sex, and Hispanic or Latino ethnicity	Civilian noninstitutional population	Civilian labor force							Not in labor force
		Total	Percent of population	Employed		Unemployed			
				Total	Percent of population	Total	Percent of labor force		
Asian									
Total, 16 years and over.......	10,751	7,202	67.0	6,917	64.3	285	4.0		3,549
16 to 19 years.................	630	157	24.9	134	21.3	23	14.6		473
20 to 24 years.................	872	526	60.3	493	56.5	33	6.3		346
25 to 54 years.................	6,615	5,408	81.8	5,223	79.0	186	3.4		1,207
55 to 64 years.................	1,343	891	66.4	856	63.8	35	3.9		452
65 years and over............	1,291	219	17.0	211	16.3	8	3.8		1,072
Women, 16 years and over...	5,639	3,350	59.4	3,225	57.2	125	3.7		2,289
16 to 19 years.................	306	72	23.6	63	20.7	9	12.3		234
20 to 24 years.................	443	258	58.2	242	54.7	16	6.1		185
25 to 54 years.................	3,426	2,488	72.6	2,405	70.2	83	3.3		938
55 to 64 years.................	726	434	59.7	418	57.6	15	3.5		293
65 years and over............	738	99	13.4	97	13.1	2	2.2		639
Men, 16 years and over.......	5,112	3,852	75.3	3,692	72.2	160	4.1		1,260
16 to 19 years.................	324	85	26.2	71	21.9	14	16.6		239
20 to 24 years.................	429	268	62.5	251	58.5	17	6.5		161
25 to 54 years.................	3,189	2,921	91.6	2,818	88.4	103	3.5		268
55 to 64 years.................	616	457	74.2	438	71.1	19	4.3		159
65 years and over............	553	120	21.8	114	20.7	6	5.1		433
Hispanic or Latino ethnicity									
Total, 16 years and over.......	32,141	22,024	68.5	20,346	63.3	1,678	7.6		10,116
16 to 19 years.................	3,042	1,121	36.9	870	28.6	251	22.4		1,921
20 to 24 years.................	3,620	2,668	73.7	2,361	65.2	307	11.5		952
25 to 54 years.................	20,030	16,117	80.5	15,110	75.4	1,007	6.2		3,913
55 to 64 years.................	2,840	1,701	59.9	1,619	57.0	81	4.8		1,139
65 years and over............	2,609	417	16.0	385	14.8	32	7.8		2,192
Women, 16 years and over...	15,616	8,769	56.2	8,098	51.9	672	7.7		6,847
16 to 19 years.................	1,489	495	33.3	391	26.2	104	21.1		994
20 to 24 years.................	1,730	1,074	62.1	955	55.2	119	11.1		655
25 to 54 years.................	9,435	6,304	66.8	5,901	62.5	403	6.4		3,131
55 to 64 years.................	1,475	722	48.9	690	46.8	32	4.4		753
65 years and over............	1,488	174	11.7	161	10.8	13	7.7		1,314
Men, 16 years and over.......	16,524	13,255	80.2	12,248	74.1	1,007	7.6		3,270
16 to 19 years.................	1,553	626	40.3	479	30.9	147	23.4		927
20 to 24 years.................	1,890	1,594	84.3	1,406	74.4	188	11.8		297
25 to 54 years.................	10,594	9,813	92.6	9,209	86.9	604	6.2		781
55 to 64 years.................	1,365	979	71.7	929	68.1	50	5.1		386
65 years and over............	1,121	243	21.7	224	20.0	19	7.8		878

SOURCE: Current Population Survey, U.S. Department of Labor, U.S. Bureau of Labor Statistics.

Table 4. **Employment status by marital status and sex, 2008 annual averages**

(Numbers in thousands)

Marital status and sex	Civilian noninsti-tutional population	Civilian labor force						Not in labor force
		Total	Percent of population	Employed		Unemployed		
				Total	Percent of population	Total	Percent of labor force	
Total								
Total, 16 years and over.....	233,788	154,287	66.0	145,362	62.2	8,924	5.8	79,501
Married, spouse present...	122,349	84,644	69.2	81,729	66.8	2,915	3.4	37,705
Unmarried, total............	111,439	69,643	62.5	63,634	57.1	6,010	8.6	41,796
Never married..............	66,254	44,874	67.7	40,452	61.1	4,422	9.9	21,381
Other marital status........	45,185	24,769	54.8	23,182	51.3	1,587	6.4	20,415
Divorced.................	22,864	16,126	70.5	15,182	66.4	944	5.9	6,738
Separated................	8,198	5,772	70.4	5,296	64.6	475	8.2	2,427
Widowed.................	14,122	2,872	20.3	2,704	19.1	168	5.9	11,251
Women								
Total, 16 years and over.....	120,675	71,767	59.5	67,876	56.2	3,891	5.4	48,908
Married, spouse present...	60,554	37,194	61.4	35,869	59.2	1,325	3.6	23,360
Unmarried, total............	60,121	34,573	57.5	32,007	53.2	2,566	7.4	25,548
Never married..............	30,980	20,231	65.3	18,513	59.8	1,717	8.5	10,749
Other marital status........	29,141	14,342	49.2	13,494	46.3	849	5.9	14,799
Divorced.................	13,379	9,222	68.9	8,743	65.4	479	5.2	4,157
Separated................	4,520	2,947	65.2	2,702	59.8	246	8.3	1,572
Widowed.................	11,242	2,173	19.3	2,048	18.2	125	5.7	9,069
Men								
Total, 16 years and over.....	113,113	82,520	73.0	77,486	68.5	5,033	6.1	30,593
Married, spouse present...	61,794	47,450	76.8	45,860	74.2	1,590	3.4	14,345
Unmarried, total............	51,318	35,070	68.3	31,627	61.6	3,443	9.8	16,248
Never married..............	35,274	24,643	69.9	21,938	62.2	2,705	11.0	10,631
Other marital status........	16,044	10,427	65.0	9,688	60.4	739	7.1	5,617
Divorced.................	9,486	6,905	72.8	6,439	67.9	465	6.7	2,581
Separated................	3,678	2,824	76.8	2,594	70.5	230	8.1	854
Widowed.................	2,880	698	24.3	655	22.7	43	6.2	2,181

SOURCE: Current Population Survey, U.S. Department of Labor, U.S. Bureau of Labor Statistics.

Table 5. **Employment status by sex, presence and age of children, race, and Hispanic or Latino ethnicity, March 2008**

(Numbers in thousands)

Characteristic	Civilian noninsti-tutional population	Civilian labor force						Not in labor force
		Total	Percent of population	Employed		Unemployed		
				Total	Percent of population	Total	Percent of labor force	
Total								
Women, 16 years and over.................	120,300	71,515	59.4	68,054	56.6	3,462	4.8	48,784
With children under 18 years old........	36,410	25,930	71.2	24,637	67.7	1,294	5.0	10,479
With children 6 to 17, none younger..	19,972	15,479	77.5	14,842	74.3	636	4.1	4,493
With children under 6 years old........	16,438	10,452	63.6	9,794	59.6	657	6.3	5,986
With children under 3 years old......	9,657	5,754	59.6	5,380	55.7	374	6.5	3,903
With no children under 18 years old...	83,890	45,585	54.3	43,417	51.8	2,168	4.8	38,305
Men, 16 years and over....................	112,695	81,576	72.4	76,737	68.1	4,839	5.9	31,119
With children under 18 years old........	27,898	26,192	93.9	25,201	90.3	991	3.8	1,706
With children 6 to 17, none younger..	15,301	14,181	92.7	13,710	89.6	471	3.3	1,119
With children under 6 years old........	12,597	12,011	95.3	11,491	91.2	520	4.3	587
With children under 3 years old......	7,514	7,198	95.8	6,871	91.4	328	4.6	316
With no children under 18 years old...	84,797	55,384	65.3	51,536	60.8	3,848	6.9	29,413
White								
Women, 16 years and over.................	96,576	57,044	59.1	54,604	56.5	2,440	4.3	39,532
With children under 18 years old........	28,428	20,085	70.7	19,213	67.6	871	4.3	8,343
With children 6 to 17, none younger..	15,697	12,115	77.2	11,678	74.4	437	3.6	3,582
With children under 6 years old........	12,731	7,970	62.6	7,536	59.2	434	5.4	4,761
With children under 3 years old......	7,544	4,458	59.1	4,207	55.8	251	5.6	3,086
With no children under 18 years old...	68,149	36,960	54.2	35,390	51.9	1,569	4.2	31,189
Men, 16 years and over....................	92,469	67,675	73.2	64,105	69.3	3,570	5.3	24,794
With children under 18 years old........	23,321	22,070	94.6	21,310	91.4	760	3.4	1,252
With children 6 to 17, none younger..	12,729	11,914	93.6	11,554	90.8	360	3.0	815
With children under 6 years old........	10,592	10,155	95.9	9,756	92.1	399	3.9	437
With children under 3 years old......	6,361	6,133	96.4	5,893	92.6	240	3.9	229
With no children under 18 years old...	69,148	45,605	66.0	42,795	61.9	2,810	6.2	23,543
Black or African American								
Women, 16 years and over.................	15,261	9,386	61.5	8,600	56.4	786	8.4	5,875
With children under 18 years old........	5,100	3,848	75.4	3,503	68.7	345	9.0	1,252
With children 6 to 17, none younger..	2,800	2,240	80.0	2,079	74.2	161	7.2	560
With children under 6 years old........	2,300	1,608	69.9	1,424	61.9	184	11.5	692
With children under 3 years old......	1,301	808	62.1	706	54.3	102	12.6	493
With no children under 18 years old...	10,160	5,538	54.5	5,097	50.2	441	8.0	4,622
Men, 16 years and over....................	12,448	8,163	65.6	7,266	58.4	898	11.0	4,285
With children under 18 years old........	2,377	2,091	88.0	1,950	82.0	142	6.8	286
With children 6 to 17, none younger..	1,401	1,196	85.4	1,134	80.9	62	5.2	205
With children under 6 years old........	976	895	91.7	816	83.6	79	8.9	81
With children under 3 years old......	553	510	92.2	456	82.4	54	10.6	43
With no children under 18 years old...	10,071	6,072	60.3	5,316	52.8	756	12.5	3,999

See note at end of table.

13

Table 5. **Employment status by sex, presence and age of children, race, and Hispanic or Latino ethnicity, March 2008—Continued**

(Numbers in thousands)

Characteristic	Civilian noninstitutional population	Civilian labor force						Not in labor force
		Total	Percent of population	Employed		Unemployed		
				Total	Percent of population	Total	Percent of labor force	
Asian								
Women, 16 years and over..................	5,580	3,384	60.7	3,271	58.6	113	3.3	2,195
With children under 18 years old........	1,899	1,321	69.6	1,279	67.3	43	3.2	578
With children 6 to 17, none younger..	1,005	756	75.2	731	72.8	24	3.2	249
With children under 6 years old........	895	566	63.2	547	61.2	18	3.2	329
With children under 3 years old......	513	314	61.3	306	59.7	8	2.6	198
With no children under 18 years old...	3,680	2,063	56.1	1,993	54.1	70	3.4	1,617
Men, 16 years and over....................	4,992	3,753	75.2	3,607	72.3	146	3.9	1,239
With children under 18 years old........	1,522	1,424	93.6	1,387	91.1	37	2.6	97
With children 6 to 17, none younger..	840	786	93.6	765	91.0	22	2.8	54
With children under 6 years old........	681	638	93.6	622	91.3	16	2.5	43
With children under 3 years old......	396	372	93.9	361	91.2	11	2.8	24
With no children under 18 years old...	3,470	2,328	67.1	2,220	64.0	108	4.6	1,142
Hispanic or Latino ethnicity								
Women, 16 years and over................	15,465	8,708	56.3	8,115	52.5	593	6.8	6,757
With children under 18 years old........	6,820	4,165	61.1	3,891	57.0	274	6.6	2,655
With children 6 to 17, none younger..	3,370	2,359	70.0	2,225	66.0	134	5.7	1,011
With children under 6 years old........	3,450	1,806	52.3	1,666	48.3	140	7.8	1,644
With children under 3 years old......	1,996	945	47.3	859	43.0	87	9.2	1,051
With no children under 18 years old...	8,645	4,543	52.5	4,224	48.9	319	7.0	4,102
Men, 16 years and over....................	16,355	13,046	79.8	12,002	73.4	1,045	8.0	3,309
With children under 18 years old........	5,072	4,780	94.2	4,518	89.1	262	5.5	292
With children 6 to 17, none younger..	2,393	2,219	92.7	2,109	88.1	111	5.0	174
With children under 6 years old........	2,679	2,561	95.6	2,409	89.9	151	5.9	118
With children under 3 years old......	1,578	1,516	96.1	1,424	90.2	92	6.1	62
With no children under 18 years old...	11,283	8,267	73.3	7,484	66.3	783	9.5	3,017

NOTE: Children are "own" children and include sons, daughters, stepchildren, and adopted children. Not included are nieces, nephews, grandchildren, and other related and unrelated children. Estimates for the above race groups (white, black or African American, and Asian) do not sum to totals because data are not presented for all races. Persons whose ethnicity is identified as Hispanic or Latino may be of any race.

SOURCE: 2008 Annual Social and Economic Supplement, Current Population Survey, U.S. Department of Labor, U.S. Bureau of Labor Statistics.

Table 6. **Employment status of women by presence and age of youngest child, marital status, race, and Hispanic or Latino ethnicity, March 2008**

(Numbers in thousands)

Presence and age of children	Civilian noninsti-tutional population	Civilian labor force						Not in labor force
		Total	Percent of population	Employed		Unemployed		
				Total	Percent of population	Total	Percent of labor force	
Total, all marital statuses								
Total, 16 years and over....................	120,300	71,515	59.4	68,054	56.6	3,462	4.8	48,784
With children under 18 years old...........	36,410	25,930	71.2	24,637	67.7	1,294	5.0	10,479
With children 6 to 17 years old,								
none younger....................	19,972	15,479	77.5	14,842	74.3	636	4.1	4,493
With children under 6 years old...........	16,438	10,452	63.6	9,794	59.6	657	6.3	5,986
With children under 3 years old.........	9,657	5,754	59.6	5,380	55.7	374	6.5	3,903
With no children under 18 years old.......	83,890	45,585	54.3	43,417	51.8	2,168	4.8	38,305
Total, married, spouse present								
Total, 16 years and over....................	60,108	37,074	61.7	35,919	59.8	1,155	3.1	23,034
With children under 18 years old...........	25,754	17,886	69.4	17,269	67.1	616	3.4	7,868
With children 6 to 17 years old,								
none younger....................	13,919	10,601	76.2	10,270	73.8	331	3.1	3,318
With children under 6 years old...........	11,835	7,285	61.6	6,999	59.1	285	3.9	4,551
With children under 3 years old.........	7,091	4,146	58.5	3,981	56.1	165	4.0	2,945
With no children under 18 years old.......	34,354	19,188	55.9	18,650	54.3	539	2.8	15,166
Total, other marital statuses[1]								
Total, 16 years and over....................	60,192	34,441	57.2	32,135	53.4	2,307	6.7	25,750
With children under 18 years old...........	10,656	8,045	75.5	7,367	69.1	677	8.4	2,611
With children 6 to 17 years old,								
none younger....................	6,053	4,878	80.6	4,573	75.5	305	6.3	1,176
With children under 6 years old...........	4,603	3,167	68.8	2,795	60.7	372	11.7	1,436
With children under 3 years old.........	2,566	1,608	62.7	1,399	54.5	209	13.0	958
With no children under 18 years old.......	49,536	26,397	53.3	24,767	50.0	1,629	6.2	23,139
White, all marital statuses								
Total, 16 years and over....................	96,576	57,044	59.1	54,604	56.5	2,440	4.3	39,532
With children under 18 years old...........	28,428	20,085	70.7	19,213	67.6	871	4.3	8,343
With children 6 to 17 years old,								
none younger....................	15,697	12,115	77.2	11,678	74.4	437	3.6	3,582
With children under 6 years old...........	12,731	7,970	62.6	7,536	59.2	434	5.4	4,761
With children under 3 years old.........	7,544	4,458	59.1	4,207	55.8	251	5.6	3,086
With no children under 18 years old.......	68,149	36,960	54.2	35,390	51.9	1,569	4.2	31,189
White, married, spouse present								
Total, 16 years and over....................	51,326	31,375	61.1	30,442	59.3	933	3.0	19,951
With children under 18 years old...........	21,566	14,870	69.0	14,381	66.7	489	3.3	6,696
With children 6 to 17 years old,								
none younger....................	11,636	8,817	75.8	8,552	73.5	265	3.0	2,819
With children under 6 years old...........	9,929	6,053	61.0	5,830	58.7	223	3.7	3,876
With children under 3 years old.........	6,005	3,504	58.4	3,376	56.2	128	3.7	2,501
With no children under 18 years old.......	29,760	16,505	55.5	16,061	54.0	445	2.7	13,255
White, other marital statuses[1]								
Total, 16 years and over....................	45,250	25,669	56.7	24,162	53.4	1,507	5.9	19,581
With children under 18 years old...........	6,862	5,215	76.0	4,832	70.4	383	7.3	1,647
With children 6 to 17 years old,								
none younger....................	4,060	3,298	81.2	3,126	77.0	172	5.2	763
With children under 6 years old...........	2,801	1,917	68.4	1,706	60.9	211	11.0	884
With children under 3 years old.........	1,539	954	62.0	831	54.0	123	12.9	585
With no children under 18 years old.......	38,388	20,454	53.3	19,330	50.4	1,124	5.5	17,934

See footnote at end of table.

Table 6. **Employment status of women by presence and age of youngest child, marital status, race, and Hispanic or Latino ethnicity, March 2008—Continued**

(Numbers in thousands)

Presence and age of children	Civilian noninsti-tutional population	Civilian labor force						Not in labor force
		Total	Percent of population	Employed		Unemployed		
				Total	Percent of population	Total	Percent of labor force	
Black or African American, all marital statuses								
Total, 16 years and over............	15,261	9,386	61.5	8,600	56.4	786	8.4	5,875
With children under 18 years old...........	5,100	3,848	75.4	3,503	68.7	345	9.0	1,252
With children 6 to 17 years old, none younger..................	2,800	2,240	80.0	2,079	74.2	161	7.2	560
With children under 6 years old...........	2,300	1,608	69.9	1,424	61.9	184	11.5	692
With children under 3 years old..........	1,301	808	62.1	706	54.3	102	12.6	493
With no children under 18 years old.......	10,160	5,538	54.5	5,097	50.2	441	8.0	4,622
Black or African American, married, spouse present								
Total, 16 years and over............	4,298	2,897	67.4	2,764	64.3	133	4.6	1,402
With children under 18 years old...........	1,912	1,473	77.0	1,394	72.9	79	5.4	439
With children 6 to 17 years old, none younger..................	1,117	923	82.6	885	79.3	38	4.1	194
With children under 6 years old...........	795	550	69.1	508	63.9	41	7.5	246
With children under 3 years old...........	442	263	59.5	238	54.0	24	9.3	179
With no children under 18 years old.......	2,386	1,424	59.7	1,370	57.4	54	3.8	962
Black or African American, other marital statuses[1]								
Total, 16 years and over............	10,962	6,489	59.2	5,836	53.2	653	10.1	4,473
With children under 18 years old...........	3,188	2,375	74.5	2,109	66.2	266	11.2	813
With children 6 to 17 years old, none younger..................	1,683	1,317	78.2	1,194	70.9	123	9.3	367
With children under 6 years old...........	1,505	1,058	70.3	915	60.8	143	13.5	446
With children under 3 years old..........	859	545	63.5	468	54.4	78	14.2	314
With no children under 18 years old.......	7,774	4,114	52.9	3,727	47.9	387	9.4	3,660
Asian, all marital statuses								
Total, 16 years and over............	5,580	3,384	60.7	3,271	58.6	113	3.3	2,195
With children under 18 years old...........	1,899	1,321	69.6	1,279	67.3	43	3.2	578
With children 6 to 17 years old, none younger..................	1,005	756	75.2	731	72.8	24	3.2	249
With children under 6 years old...........	895	566	63.2	547	61.2	18	3.2	329
With children under 3 years old..........	513	314	61.3	306	59.7	8	2.6	198
With no children under 18 years old.......	3,680	2,063	56.1	1,993	54.1	70	3.4	1,617
Asian, married, spouse present								
Total, 16 years and over............	3,293	2,064	62.7	2,009	61.0	55	2.6	1,229
With children under 18 years old...........	1,656	1,119	67.6	1,087	65.7	31	2.8	537
With children 6 to 17 years old, none younger..................	874	640	73.3	619	70.8	21	3.3	234
With children under 6 years old...........	782	478	61.2	468	59.9	10	2.1	303
With children under 3 years old..........	452	269	59.5	263	58.1	6	2.4	183
With no children under 18 years old.......	1,637	945	57.7	922	56.3	23	2.5	692
Asian, other marital statuses[1]								
Total, 16 years and over............	2,287	1,320	57.7	1,262	55.2	59	4.4	966
With children under 18 years old...........	244	203	83.2	191	78.6	11	5.5	41
With children 6 to 17 years old, none younger..................	131	116	88.2	112	85.8	3	2.7	15
With children under 6 years old...........	113	87	77.3	79	70.2	8	9.2	26
With children under 3 years old..........	60	45	74.9	43	72.0	2	3.9	15
With no children under 18 years old.......	2,043	1,118	54.7	1,070	52.4	47	4.2	925

See footnote at end of table.

Table 6. **Employment status of women by presence and age of youngest child, marital status, race, and Hispanic or Latino ethnicity, March 2008—Continued**

(Numbers in thousands)

Presence and age of children	Civilian noninsti-tutional population	Civilian labor force						Not in labor force
		Total	Percent of population	Employed		Unemployed		
				Total	Percent of population	Total	Percent of labor force	
Hispanic or Latino, all marital statuses								
Total, 16 years and over......................	15,465	8,708	56.3	8,115	52.5	593	6.8	6,757
With children under 18 years old...........	6,820	4,165	61.1	3,891	57.0	274	6.6	2,655
With children 6 to 17 years old,								
none younger..................................	3,370	2,359	70.0	2,225	66.0	134	5.7	1,011
With children under 6 years old...........	3,450	1,806	52.3	1,666	48.3	140	7.8	1,644
With children under 3 years old.........	1,996	945	47.3	859	43.0	87	9.2	1,051
With no children under 18 years old.......	8,645	4,543	52.5	4,224	48.9	319	7.0	4,102
Hispanic or Latino, married, spouse present								
Total, 16 years and over......................	7,557	4,103	54.3	3,874	51.3	229	5.6	3,454
With children under 18 years old...........	4,663	2,625	56.3	2,482	53.2	143	5.4	2,038
With children 6 to 17 years old,								
none younger..................................	2,259	1,482	65.6	1,414	62.6	67	4.5	778
With children under 6 years old...........	2,403	1,143	47.6	1,067	44.4	76	6.6	1,260
With children under 3 years old.........	1,407	614	43.6	564	40.1	50	8.1	793
With no children under 18 years old.......	2,894	1,479	51.1	1,393	48.1	86	5.8	1,415
Hispanic or Latino, other marital statuses[1]								
Total, 16 years and over......................	7,908	4,605	58.2	4,241	53.6	364	7.9	3,304
With children under 18 years old...........	2,157	1,540	71.4	1,409	65.3	131	8.5	617
With children 6 to 17 years old,								
none younger..................................	1,110	877	79.0	810	73.0	67	7.6	233
With children under 6 years old...........	1,047	663	63.3	599	57.2	64	9.7	384
With children under 3 years old.........	589	331	56.2	294	49.9	37	11.1	258
With no children under 18 years old.......	5,751	3,064	53.3	2,832	49.2	233	7.6	2,687

[1] Includes never-married, divorced, separated, and widowed persons.

NOTE: Children are "own" children and include sons, daughters, stepchildren, and adopted children. Not included are nieces, nephews, grandchildren, and other related and unrelated children. Detail for the above race groups (white,

black or African American, and Asian) do not sum to totals because data are not presented for all races. Persons whose ethnicity is identified as Hispanic or Latino may be of any race.

SOURCE: 2008 Annual Social and Economic Supplement, Current Population Survey, U.S. Department of Labor, U.S. Bureau of Labor Statistics.

Table 7. **Employment status of women by presence and age of youngest child, March 1975-2008**

(Numbers in thousands)

Year	With children under age 18					With children ages 6 to 17, none younger				
	Civilian labor force		Employed	Unemployed		Civilian labor force		Employed	Unemployed	
	Total	Percent of population		Total	Percent of labor force	Total	Percent of population		Total	Percent of labor force
1975......	14,616	47.4	13,069	1,548	11.0	8,917	54.9	8,218	700	7.9
1976......	15,073	48.8	13,725	1,346	8.9	9,388	56.2	8,769	621	6.6
1977......	15,669	50.8	14,276	1,393	8.9	10,040	58.3	9,389	650	6.5
1978......	16,385	53.0	15,142	1,242	7.6	10,401	60.0	9,845	556	5.3
1979......	16,883	54.5	15,624	1,259	7.7	10,646	61.6	10,030	615	5.8
1980......	17,790	56.6	16,526	1,264	7.1	11,252	64.3	10,640	612	5.4
1981......	18,422	58.1	16,952	1,471	8.0	11,490	65.5	10,725	765	6.7
1982......	18,744	58.5	16,854	1,890	10.1	11,377	65.8	10,440	936	8.2
1983......	18,924	58.9	16,792	2,131	11.3	11,340	66.3	10,303	1,037	9.1
1984......	19,555	60.5	17,782	1,773	9.1	11,538	68.1	10,739	799	6.9
1985......	20,041	62.1	18,306	1,735	8.7	11,826	69.9	10,984	842	7.1
1986......	20,620	62.8	18,922	1,698	8.2	12,075	70.4	11,320	756	6.3
1987......	21,422	64.7	19,798	1,624	7.6	12,438	72.0	11,661	778	6.3
1988......	21,545	65.1	20,141	1,404	6.5	12,683	73.3	12,042	641	5.1
1989......	21,936	65.7	20,647	1,289	5.9	12,800	74.2	12,168	632	4.9
1990......	22,196	66.7	20,865	1,331	6.0	12,799	74.7	12,133	666	5.2
1991......	22,327	66.6	20,774	1,552	7.0	12,691	74.4	12,017	674	5.3
1992......	22,756	67.2	21,052	1,704	7.5	13,183	75.9	12,391	793	6.0
1993......	23,063	66.9	21,521	1,541	6.7	13,441	75.4	12,757	684	5.1
1994......	24,191	68.4	22,467	1,724	7.1	13,863	76.0	13,074	789	5.7
1995......	24,695	69.7	23,195	1,500	6.1	14,300	76.4	13,608	691	4.8
1996......	24,720	70.2	23,386	1,334	5.4	14,427	77.2	13,794	633	4.4
1997......	25,604	72.1	24,082	1,522	5.9	14,993	78.1	14,282	711	4.7
1998......	25,647	72.3	24,209	1,438	5.6	15,028	78.4	14,370	658	4.4
1999......	25,472	72.1	24,307	1,165	4.6	15,150	78.5	14,633	516	3.4
2000......	25,795	72.9	24,693	1,102	4.3	15,479	79.0	14,931	549	3.5
2001......	26,269	72.7	25,030	1,239	4.7	15,839	79.4	15,220	619	3.9
2002......	26,140	72.2	24,612	1,529	5.8	15,948	78.6	15,171	777	4.9
2003......	26,202	71.7	24,598	1,603	6.1	15,993	78.7	15,166	828	5.2
2004......	25,913	70.7	24,413	1,501	5.8	15,782	77.5	15,006	776	4.9
2005......	25,941	70.5	24,564	1,377	5.3	15,594	76.9	14,930	663	4.3
2006......	26,009	70.6	24,728	1,281	4.9	15,579	76.9	14,949	630	4.0
2007......	26,834	71.3	25,646	1,188	4.4	15,940	77.7	15,341	599	3.8
2008......	25,930	71.2	24,637	1,294	5.0	15,479	77.5	14,842	636	4.1

See note at end of table.

Table 7. **Employment status of women by presence and age of youngest child, March 1975-2008—Continued**

(Numbers in thousands)

Year	With children under age 6					With children under age 3				
	Civilian labor force		Employed	Unemployed		Civilian labor force		Employed	Unemployed	
	Total	Percent of population		Total	Percent of labor force	Total	Percent of population		Total	Percent of labor force
1975......	5,699	39.0	4,851	848	14.9	2,824	34.3	2,326	500	17.7
1976......	5,684	40.1	4,957	727	12.8	2,702	34.1	2,285	418	15.5
1977......	5,629	41.2	4,887	742	13.2	2,795	35.4	2,371	424	15.2
1978......	5,983	44.0	5,297	687	11.5	3,179	39.4	2,768	411	12.9
1979......	6,238	45.7	5,594	644	10.3	3,380	41.1	2,979	401	11.9
1980......	6,538	46.8	5,886	652	10.0	3,565	41.9	3,167	398	11.2
1981......	6,933	48.9	6,227	706	10.2	3,826	44.3	3,380	446	11.7
1982......	7,367	49.9	6,414	953	12.9	4,133	45.6	3,542	591	14.3
1983......	7,583	50.5	6,489	1,094	14.4	4,233	46.0	3,551	682	16.1
1984......	8,017	52.1	7,043	974	12.1	4,401	47.6	3,839	562	12.8
1985......	8,215	53.5	7,322	893	10.9	4,601	49.5	4,089	513	11.1
1986......	8,545	54.4	7,602	943	11.0	4,786	50.8	4,227	559	11.7
1987......	8,983	56.7	8,137	846	9.4	5,064	52.9	4,570	494	9.8
1988......	8,862	56.1	8,099	763	8.6	4,947	52.4	4,477	470	9.5
1989......	9,136	56.7	8,478	657	7.2	5,053	52.4	4,671	381	7.5
1990......	9,397	58.2	8,732	664	7.1	5,216	53.6	4,823	393	7.5
1991......	9,636	58.4	8,758	878	9.1	5,417	54.5	4,868	550	10.1
1992......	9,573	58.0	8,662	911	9.5	5,329	54.5	4,776	553	10.4
1993......	9,621	57.9	8,764	857	8.9	5,349	53.9	4,857	492	9.2
1994......	10,328	60.3	9,394	935	9.0	5,724	57.1	5,165	559	9.8
1995......	10,395	62.3	9,587	809	7.8	5,650	58.7	5,172	478	8.5
1996......	10,293	62.3	9,592	701	6.8	5,619	59.0	5,222	397	7.1
1997......	10,610	65.0	9,800	810	7.6	5,839	61.8	5,366	473	8.1
1998......	10,619	65.2	9,839	780	7.3	5,882	62.2	5,454	428	7.3
1999......	10,322	64.4	9,674	648	6.3	5,645	60.7	5,285	359	6.4
2000......	10,316	65.3	9,763	553	5.4	5,670	61.0	5,350	320	5.6
2001......	10,430	64.4	9,810	620	5.9	5,743	60.7	5,350	393	6.8
2002......	10,193	64.1	9,441	752	7.4	5,600	60.5	5,160	440	7.9
2003......	10,209	62.9	9,433	776	7.6	5,568	58.7	5,112	456	8.2
2004......	10,131	62.2	9,407	724	7.1	5,401	57.3	4,983	417	7.7
2005......	10,347	62.6	9,634	714	6.9	5,704	58.9	5,299	405	7.1
2006......	10,430	63.0	9,779	651	6.2	5,842	59.9	5,458	384	6.6
2007......	10,894	63.5	10,305	589	5.4	6,006	60.1	5,679	327	5.5
2008......	10,452	63.6	9,794	657	6.3	5,754	59.6	5,380	374	6.5

See note at end of table.

Table 7. **Employment status of women by presence and age of youngest child, March 1975-2008—Continued**

(Numbers in thousands)

| Year | With no children under age 18 | | | | |
| | Civilian labor force | | Employed | Unemployed | |
	Total	Percent of population		Total	Percent of labor force
1975.......	22,365	45.1	20,381	1,984	8.9
1976.......	23,327	45.7	21,389	1,938	8.3
1977.......	24,385	46.4	22,348	2,037	8.4
1978.......	25,362	47.0	23,631	1,731	6.8
1979.......	26,962	48.6	25,285	1,677	6.2
1980.......	27,144	48.1	25,375	1,769	6.5
1981.......	27,992	48.7	25,934	2,059	7.4
1982.......	28,351	48.6	26,041	2,311	8.2
1983.......	28,856	48.7	26,373	2,483	8.6
1984.......	29,684	49.3	27,652	2,032	6.8
1985.......	30,850	50.4	28,814	2,036	6.6
1986.......	31,112	50.5	29,107	2,005	6.4
1987.......	31,538	50.5	29,688	1,850	5.9
1988.......	32,490	51.2	30,911	1,580	4.9
1989.......	33,255	51.9	31,761	1,495	4.5
1990.......	33,942	52.3	32,391	1,551	4.6
1991.......	34,047	52.0	32,167	1,880	5.5
1992.......	34,487	52.3	32,481	2,006	5.8
1993.......	34,495	52.1	32,476	2,020	5.9
1994.......	35,455	53.1	33,345	2,110	6.0
1995.......	35,843	52.9	34,054	1,789	5.0
1996.......	36,509	53.0	34,698	1,811	5.0
1997.......	37,295	53.6	35,572	1,723	4.6
1998.......	38,253	54.1	36,680	1,573	4.1
1999.......	39,314	54.3	37,587	1,727	4.4
2000.......	40,142	54.8	38,408	1,733	4.3
2001.......	40,996	54.4	39,363	1,633	4.0
2002.......	41,278	54.0	39,038	2,241	5.4
2003.......	42,039	54.1	39,667	2,372	5.6
2004.......	42,289	53.8	40,000	2,289	5.4
2005.......	42,677	53.5	40,570	2,107	4.9
2006.......	43,392	53.6	41,440	1,952	4.5
2007.......	44,039	53.9	42,279	1,760	4.0
2008.......	45,585	54.3	43,417	2,168	4.8

NOTE: Children are "own" children and include sons, daughters, stepchildren, and adopted children. Not included are nieces, nephews, grandchildren, and other related and unrelated children. Data for 1994 and subsequent years are not directly comparable with data for 1993 and earlier years because of the introduction of a major redesign of the Current Population Survey.

SOURCE: 2008 Annual Social and Economic Supplement, Current Population Survey, U.S. Department of Labor, U.S. Bureau of Labor Statistics.

Table 8. **Employment status of the civilian noninstitutional population 25 to 64 years of age by educational attainment and sex, 2008 annual averages**

(Numbers in thousands)

Educational attainment and sex	Civilian noninstitutional population	Civilian labor force						Not in labor force
		Total	Percent of population	Employed		Unemployed		
				Total	Percent of population	Total	Percent of labor force	
Total								
Total, 25 to 64 years........................	159,142	126,011	79.2	120,181	75.5	5,830	4.6	33,131
Less than a high school diploma........	17,959	11,400	63.5	10,353	57.6	1,047	9.2	6,559
High school graduates, no college[1]....	47,528	36,263	76.3	34,181	71.9	2,082	5.7	11,265
Some college or associate degree.....	43,487	35,251	81.1	33,639	77.4	1,612	4.6	8,236
College graduates, total..................	50,168	43,097	85.9	42,008	83.7	1,089	2.5	7,071
Bachelor's degree.........................	33,175	28,214	85.0	27,445	82.7	769	2.7	4,961
Master's degree............................	12,454	10,775	86.5	10,531	84.6	244	2.3	1,679
Professional degree......................	2,550	2,306	90.4	2,267	88.9	40	1.7	244
Doctoral degree............................	1,989	1,801	90.6	1,766	88.8	35	2.0	188
Women								
Total, 25 to 64 years........................	80,941	58,465	72.2	55,858	69.0	2,607	4.5	22,476
Less than a high school diploma........	8,379	4,045	48.3	3,652	43.6	393	9.7	4,334
High school graduates, no college[1]....	23,352	15,881	68.0	15,024	64.3	857	5.4	7,471
Some college or associate degree.....	23,369	17,754	76.0	16,945	72.5	809	4.6	5,614
College graduates, total..................	25,842	20,785	80.4	20,237	78.3	548	2.6	5,057
Bachelor's degree.........................	17,230	13,605	79.0	13,219	76.7	386	2.8	3,624
Master's degree............................	6,829	5,637	82.5	5,512	80.7	124	2.2	1,192
Professional degree......................	1,023	879	85.9	860	84.1	19	2.2	144
Doctoral degree............................	760	664	87.4	646	85.0	18	2.8	96
Men								
Total, 25 to 64 years........................	78,202	67,546	86.4	64,323	82.3	3,223	4.8	10,655
Less than a high school diploma........	9,580	7,355	76.8	6,700	69.9	655	8.9	2,225
High school graduates, no college[1]....	24,176	20,382	84.3	19,157	79.2	1,225	6.0	3,794
Some college or associate degree.....	20,119	17,497	87.0	16,694	83.0	803	4.6	2,622
College graduates, total..................	24,326	22,312	91.7	21,772	89.5	540	2.4	2,014
Bachelor's degree.........................	15,945	14,608	91.6	14,226	89.2	383	2.6	1,337
Master's degree............................	5,625	5,139	91.4	5,019	89.2	120	2.3	486
Professional degree......................	1,528	1,428	93.5	1,407	92.1	21	1.5	100
Doctoral degree............................	1,229	1,137	92.5	1,120	91.2	17	1.5	92

[1] Includes persons with a high school diploma or equivalent.

SOURCE: Current Population Survey, U.S. Department of Labor, U.S. Bureau of Labor Statistics.

Table 9. **Percent distribution of the civilian labor force 25 to 64 years of age by educational attainment and sex, 1970-2008**

Year	Civilian labor force (thousands)	Percent distribution				
		Total	High school		College	
			Less than 4 years	4 years, no college	1 to 3 years	4 years or more
Total, both sexes						
1970 [1]	61,765	100.0	36.1	38.1	11.8	14.1
1971	62,344	100.0	34.5	38.4	12.3	14.8
1972	63,704	100.0	33.3	38.8	12.4	15.5
1973	64,775	100.0	30.9	39.7	13.0	16.4
1974	66,527	100.0	29.3	39.5	13.7	17.5
1975	67,774	100.0	27.5	39.7	14.4	18.3
1976	69,243	100.0	25.8	39.6	15.2	19.4
1977	71,324	100.0	24.9	39.2	15.7	20.2
1978	73,504	100.0	23.7	39.2	16.5	20.6
1979	75,781	100.0	21.8	39.5	17.3	21.3
1980	78,010	100.0	20.6	39.8	17.6	22.0
1981	80,273	100.0	19.7	40.6	17.7	22.0
1982	81,516	100.0	18.8	40.8	17.3	23.1
1983	83,615	100.0	17.8	39.9	18.1	24.2
1984	86,001	100.0	16.7	40.2	18.4	24.7
1985	88,424	100.0	15.9	40.2	19.0	24.9
1986	90,500	100.0	15.5	40.2	19.5	24.8
1987	92,966	100.0	14.9	40.2	19.7	25.3
1988	94,870	100.0	14.7	39.9	19.7	25.7
1989	97,318	100.0	14.0	39.6	20.0	26.4
1990	99,175	100.0	13.4	39.5	20.7	26.4
1991	100,480	100.0	13.0	39.4	21.1	26.5

Year	Civilian labor force (thousands)	Percent distribution				
		Total	Less than a high school diploma	High school graduates, no college [2]	Some college, no degree, or associate degree	College graduates [3]
Total, both sexes						
1992 [4]	103,018	100.0	12.1	35.7	25.6	26.6
1993	104,237	100.0	11.3	35.1	26.6	27.0
1994	105,610	100.0	10.8	33.9	27.7	27.6
1995	107,032	100.0	10.4	33.2	28.1	28.3
1996	108,932	100.0	10.6	32.9	27.8	28.7
1997	110,945	100.0	10.6	32.9	27.5	29.0
1998	111,932	100.0	10.5	32.4	27.4	29.8
1999	113,095	100.0	10.0	31.8	27.6	30.5
2000	115,750	100.0	10.1	31.4	27.8	30.7
2001	116,893	100.0	10.1	30.9	28.0	31.0
2002	118,028	100.0	10.0	30.7	27.7	31.6
2003	119,621	100.0	9.9	30.3	27.6	32.1
2004	120,135	100.0	9.7	30.1	27.7	32.4
2005	121,752	100.0	9.8	29.9	27.8	32.5
2006	123,550	100.0	9.7	29.6	27.7	33.0
2007	125,104	100.0	9.3	29.2	27.7	33.8
2008	126,011	100.0	9.0	28.8	28.0	34.2

See footnotes at end of table.

Table 9. **Percent distribution of the civilian labor force 25 to 64 years of age by educational attainment and sex, 1970-2008—Continued**

Year	Civilian labor force (thousands)	Percent distribution				
		Total	High school		College	
			Less than 4 years	4 years, no college	1 to 3 years	4 years or more
Women						
1970 [1]	22,462	100.0	33.5	44.3	10.9	11.2
1971	22,804	100.0	32.2	44.2	11.9	11.8
1972	23,606	100.0	30.7	45.1	11.8	12.4
1973	24,158	100.0	28.4	45.9	12.4	13.3
1974	25,203	100.0	26.7	45.3	13.4	14.6
1975	26,146	100.0	26.5	45.5	13.9	14.1
1976	27,166	100.0	24.0	45.1	14.7	16.2
1977	28,369	100.0	22.8	45.1	15.2	16.9
1978	29,738	100.0	22.0	44.9	16.1	17.0
1979	31,151	100.0	20.1	45.0	17.1	17.8
1980	32,593	100.0	18.4	45.4	17.4	18.7
1981	33,910	100.0	17.4	46.1	17.9	18.6
1982	34,870	100.0	16.6	45.6	18.3	19.5
1983	35,712	100.0	15.6	44.8	18.8	20.9
1984	37,234	100.0	14.5	44.9	18.9	21.7
1985	38,779	100.0	13.7	44.4	19.9	22.0
1986	39,767	100.0	13.2	44.3	20.3	22.2
1987	41,105	100.0	12.5	44.0	20.7	22.8
1988	42,254	100.0	12.4	43.3	21.2	23.1
1989	43,650	100.0	11.9	42.9	20.9	24.3
1990	44,699	100.0	11.3	42.4	21.9	24.5
1991	45,315	100.0	10.9	41.6	22.2	25.2

Year	Civilian labor force (thousands)	Percent distribution			
		Total	Less than a high school diploma	High school graduates, no college[2]	Some college, no degree, or associate degree	College graduates[3]
Women						
1992 [4]	46,589	100.0	10.3	37.4	27.3	25.0
1993	47,245	100.0	9.3	36.6	28.4	25.7
1994	48,405	100.0	9.0	35.0	29.8	26.2
1995	49,247	100.0	8.8	34.1	30.2	26.9
1996	50,240	100.0	8.8	33.6	29.9	27.8
1997	51,261	100.0	8.7	33.5	29.4	28.4
1998	51,678	100.0	8.8	32.7	29.4	29.2
1999	52,525	100.0	8.5	32.1	29.5	29.9
2000	53,749	100.0	8.5	31.6	29.8	30.1
2001	54,229	100.0	8.4	31.0	30.2	30.4
2002	54,710	100.0	8.1	30.6	29.9	31.3
2003	55,596	100.0	7.9	30.0	29.9	32.2
2004	55,616	100.0	7.7	29.4	30.2	32.6
2005	56,322	100.0	7.7	28.7	30.2	33.3
2006	57,201	100.0	7.6	28.3	30.2	33.9
2007	57,791	100.0	7.1	27.9	30.1	34.9
2008	58,465	100.0	6.9	27.2	30.4	35.6

See footnotes at end of table.

Table 9. **Percent distribution of the civilian labor force 25 to 64 years of age by educational attainment and sex, 1970-2008—Continued**

Year	Civilian labor force (thousands)	Percent distribution					
		Total	High school		College	
			Less than 4 years	4 years, no college	1 to 3 years	4 years or more
Men						
1970 [1]..........	39,303	100.0	37.5	34.5	12.2	15.7
1971..............	39,539	100.0	35.9	35.1	12.5	16.5
1972..............	40,098	100.0	34.8	35.1	12.8	17.3
1973..............	40,617	100.0	32.4	36.0	13.4	18.2
1974..............	41,344	100.0	30.8	36.0	13.9	19.3
1975..............	41,628	100.0	28.9	36.1	14.8	20.2
1976..............	42,077	100.0	27.0	36.0	15.5	21.5
1977..............	42,954	100.0	26.3	35.3	16.1	22.3
1978..............	43,766	100.0	24.8	35.3	16.9	23.0
1979..............	44,630	100.0	23.0	35.7	17.5	23.8
1980..............	45,417	100.0	22.2	35.7	17.7	24.3
1981..............	46,363	100.0	21.5	36.5	17.4	24.6
1982..............	47,144	100.0	20.3	36.8	17.5	25.5
1983..............	47,903	100.0	19.4	36.3	17.7	26.6
1984..............	48,767	100.0	18.4	36.7	18.0	26.9
1985..............	49,647	100.0	17.7	36.9	18.3	27.1
1986..............	50,733	100.0	17.2	37.0	18.9	26.9
1987..............	51,860	100.0	16.8	37.1	18.9	27.2
1988..............	52,616	100.0	16.5	37.3	18.5	27.8
1989..............	53,668	100.0	15.7	36.9	19.2	28.2
1990..............	54,476	100.0	15.1	37.2	19.7	28.0
1991..............	55,165	100.0	14.7	37.5	20.2	27.6

See footnotes at end of table.

Table 9. **Percent distribution of the civilian labor force 25 to 64 years of age by educational attainment and sex, 1970-2008—Continued**

Year	Civilian labor force (thousands)	Percent distribution				
		Total	Less than a high school diploma	High school graduates, no college[2]	Some college, no degree, or associate degree	College graduates[3]
Men						
1992[4].............	56,428	100.0	13.7	34.2	24.3	27.8
1993..............	56,992	100.0	12.9	33.9	25.1	28.1
1994..............	57,205	100.0	12.4	33.0	25.9	28.8
1995..............	57,784	100.0	11.8	32.4	26.3	29.4
1996..............	58,692	100.0	12.2	32.3	26.1	29.4
1997..............	59,684	100.0	12.2	32.4	25.9	29.6
1998..............	60,255	100.0	12.0	32.1	25.6	30.3
1999..............	60,570	100.0	11.4	31.6	26.0	31.0
2000..............	62,001	100.0	11.5	31.2	26.1	31.2
2001..............	62,664	100.0	11.5	30.9	26.2	31.4
2002..............	63,318	100.0	11.6	30.8	25.8	31.8
2003..............	64,025	100.0	11.7	30.6	25.6	32.1
2004..............	64,519	100.0	11.5	30.7	25.6	32.3
2005..............	65,430	100.0	11.5	30.9	25.7	31.9
2006..............	66,350	100.0	11.5	30.6	25.5	32.3
2007..............	67,313	100.0	11.2	30.4	25.6	32.9
2008..............	67,546	100.0	10.9	30.2	25.9	33.0

[1] Data from 1970-1991 are based on the March Current Population Survey.

[2] Includes persons with a high school diploma or equivalent.

[3] Includes persons with bachelor's, master's, professional, and doctoral degrees.

[4] Beginning in 1992, data on educational attainment are annual averages and are based on the highest diploma or degree received rather than the number of years of school completed.

SOURCE: Current Population Survey, U.S. Department of Labor, U.S. Bureau of Labor Statistics.

Table 10. **Employed persons by major occupation and sex, 2007 and 2008 annual averages**

(Numbers in thousands)

Occupation and sex	Year			
	2007		2008	
	Number	Percent	Number	Percent
Total				
Total, 16 years and over..	146,047	100.0	145,362	100.0
Management, professional, and related occupations	51,788	35.5	52,761	36.3
Management, business, and financial operations occupations	21,577	14.8	22,059	15.2
Professional and related occupations	30,210	20.7	30,702	21.1
Service occupations	24,137	16.5	24,451	16.8
Sales and office occupations	36,212	24.8	35,544	24.5
Sales and related occupations	16,698	11.4	16,295	11.2
Office and administrative support occupations	19,513	13.4	19,249	13.2
Natural resources, construction, and maintenance occupations	15,740	10.8	14,806	10.2
Farming, fishing, and forestry occupations	960	.7	988	.7
Construction and extraction occupations	9,535	6.5	8,667	6.0
Installation, maintenance, and repair occupations	5,245	3.6	5,152	3.5
Production, transportation, and material moving occupations	18,171	12.4	17,800	12.2
Production occupations	9,395	6.4	8,973	6.2
Transportation and material moving occupations	8,776	6.0	8,827	6.1
Women				
Total, 16 years and over..	67,792	100.0	67,876	100.0
Management, professional, and related occupations	26,195	38.6	26,813	39.5
Management, business, and financial operations occupations	9,203	13.6	9,412	13.9
Professional and related occupations	16,992	25.1	17,401	25.6
Service occupations	13,800	20.4	13,980	20.6
Sales and office occupations	22,948	33.8	22,477	33.1
Sales and related occupations	8,275	12.2	8,073	11.9
Office and administrative support occupations	14,673	21.6	14,404	21.2
Natural resources, construction, and maintenance occupations	662	1.0	626	.9
Farming, fishing, and forestry occupations	201	.3	208	.3
Construction and extraction occupations	258	.4	219	.3
Installation, maintenance, and repair occupations	202	.3	199	.3
Production, transportation, and material moving occupations	4,188	6.2	3,980	5.9
Production occupations	2,832	4.2	2,661	3.9
Transportation and material moving occupations	1,355	2.0	1,319	1.9

Table 10. **Employed persons by major occupation and sex, 2007 and 2008 annual averages—Continued**

(Numbers in thousands)

Occupation	Year			
	2007		2008	
	Number	Percent	Number	Percent
Men				
Total, 16 years and over..	78,254	100.0	77,486	100.0
Management, professional, and related occupations	25,593	32.7	25,948	33.5
Management, business, and financial operations occupations	12,375	15.8	12,647	16.3
Professional and related occupations	13,218	16.9	13,301	17.2
Service occupations	10,337	13.2	10,471	13.5
Sales and office occupations	13,264	16.9	13,067	16.9
Sales and related occupations	8,424	10.8	8,221	10.6
Office and administrative support occupations	4,840	6.2	4,845	6.3
Natural resources, construction, and maintenance occupations	15,078	19.3	14,181	18.3
Farming, fishing, and forestry occupations	759	1.0	780	1.0
Construction and extraction occupations	9,276	11.9	8,448	10.9
Installation, maintenance, and repair occupations	5,043	6.4	4,953	6.4
Production, transportation, and material moving occupations	13,983	17.9	13,820	17.8
Production occupations	6,563	8.4	6,313	8.1
Transportation and material moving occupations	7,420	9.5	7,507	9.7

SOURCE: Current Population Survey, U.S. Department of Labor, U.S. Bureau of Labor Statistics.

Table 11. **Employed persons by detailed occupation and sex, 2008 annual averages**

(Numbers in thousands)

Occupation	Total employed	Percent women
Total, 16 years and over..	145,362	46.7
Management, professional, and related occupations..	52,761	50.8
Management, business, and financial operations occupations................................	22,059	42.7
Management occupations...	15,852	37.4
Chief executives..	1,655	23.4
General and operations managers..	985	30.1
Legislators..	23	-
Advertising and promotions managers...	77	62.1
Marketing and sales managers...	922	42.0
Public relations managers..	64	60.3
Administrative services managers...	100	32.6
Computer and information systems managers...	475	27.2
Financial managers...	1,168	54.8
Human resources managers..	293	66.3
Industrial production managers..	243	14.5
Purchasing managers..	193	40.4
Transportation, storage, and distribution managers.................................	239	17.0
Farm, ranch, and other agricultural managers.......................................	217	23.9
Farmers and ranchers...	751	24.4
Construction managers..	1,244	8.2
Education administrators..	829	65.1
Engineering managers...	109	6.3
Food service managers..	1,039	44.8
Funeral directors..	45	-
Gaming managers...	18	-
Lodging managers..	177	46.7
Medical and health services managers...	561	69.4
Natural sciences managers...	15	-
Postmasters and mail superintendents...	41	-
Property, real estate, and community association managers........................	558	49.6
Social and community service managers...	338	68.1
Managers, all other...	3,473	35.8
Business and financial operations occupations..	6,207	56.2
Agents and business managers of artists, performers, and athletes..............	50	36.5
Purchasing agents and buyers, farm products..	6	-
Wholesale and retail buyers, except farm products..................................	191	47.6
Purchasing agents, except wholesale, retail, and farm products..................	264	56.5
Claims adjusters, appraisers, examiners, and investigators........................	312	65.7
Compliance officers, except agriculture, construction, health and safety, and transportation...	179	52.3
Cost estimators...	100	10.0
Human resources, training, and labor relations specialists.........................	803	70.7
Logisticians..	50	47.2
Management analysts..	731	43.5
Meeting and convention planners...	55	79.2
Other business operations specialists..	254	66.3
Accountants and auditors...	1,762	61.1
Appraisers and assessors of real estate...	102	33.4
Budget analysts...	64	57.1
Credit analysts..	20	-
Financial analysts..	110	38.8

See note at end of table.

(Numbers in thousands)

Occupation	Total employed	Percent women
Personal financial advisors..	430	34.3
Insurance underwriters..	82	80.3
Financial examiners...	7	-
Loan counselors and officers..	392	58.0
Tax examiners, collectors, and revenue agents.................	58	64.2
Tax preparers..	105	66.6
Financial specialists, all other...	78	57.0
Professional and related occupations.......................................	30,702	56.7
Computer and mathematical occupations.............................	3,676	24.8
Computer scientists and systems analysts.......................	837	27.5
Computer programmers...	534	22.4
Computer software engineers...	1,034	20.9
Computer support specialists..	382	27.7
Database administrators..	93	29.2
Network and computer systems administrators..................	227	21.4
Network systems and data communications analysts.........	422	23.7
Actuaries...	26	-
Mathematicians...	3	-
Operations research analysts..	75	47.6
Statisticians..	41	-
Miscellaneous mathematical science occupations.............	3	-
Architecture and engineering occupations............................	2,931	13.5
Architects, except naval..	233	24.8
Surveyors, cartographers, and photogrammetrists.............	49	-
Aerospace engineers..	137	10.3
Agricultural engineers...	3	-
Biomedical engineers..	9	-
Chemical engineers...	64	13.1
Civil engineers..	346	10.4
Computer hardware engineers..	69	19.4
Electrical and electronics engineers.................................	350	7.7
Environmental engineers...	37	-
Industrial engineers, including health and safety...............	177	14.9
Marine engineers and naval architects..............................	17	-
Materials engineers..	40	-
Mechanical engineers...	318	6.7
Mining and geological engineers, including mining safety engineers..............	10	-
Nuclear engineers...	9	-
Petroleum engineers...	18	-
Engineers, all other...	363	11.5
Drafters...	162	23.4
Engineering technicians, except drafters...........................	416	18.5
Surveying and mapping technicians..................................	105	4.9
Life, physical, and social science occupations......................	1,307	46.1
Agricultural and food scientists..	38	-
Biological scientists...	101	52.9
Conservation scientists and foresters................................	24	-
Medical scientists..	132	52.3
Astronomers and physicists...	19	-
Atmospheric and space scientists.....................................	10	-
Chemists and materials scientists.....................................	118	33.1

See note at end of table.

Table 11. **Employed persons by detailed occupation and sex, 2008 annual averages—Continued**

(Numbers in thousands)

Occupation	Total employed	Percent women
Environmental scientists and geoscientists...	85	29.3
Physical scientists, all other..	136	40.7
Economists..	19	-
Market and survey researchers..	134	57.0
Psychologists..	176	66.9
Sociologists..	2	-
Urban and regional planners..	32	-
Miscellaneous social scientists and related workers...	41	-
Agricultural and food science technicians..	24	-
Biological technicians..	24	-
Chemical technicians..	53	35.2
Geological and petroleum technicians..	9	-
Nuclear technicians...	3	-
Other life, physical, and social science technicians...	129	48.3
Community and social services occupations...	2,293	60.3
Counselors..	674	68.0
Social workers...	729	79.4
Miscellaneous community and social service specialists......................................	303	61.4
Clergy..	441	14.8
Directors, religious activities and education...	50	63.5
Religious workers, all other...	95	65.6
Legal occupations...	1,671	51.9
Lawyers...	1,014	34.4
Judges, magistrates, and other judicial workers..	54	43.6
Paralegals and legal assistants...	346	87.7
Miscellaneous legal support workers...	257	74.5
Education, training, and library occupations...	8,605	74.0
Postsecondary teachers..	1,218	46.1
Preschool and kindergarten teachers..	685	97.6
Elementary and middle school teachers...	2,958	81.2
Secondary school teachers..	1,210	56.0
Special education teachers..	387	84.9
Other teachers and instructors..	751	66.9
Archivists, curators, and museum technicians..	35	-
Librarians..	197	83.5
Library technicians..	44	-
Teacher assistants..	1,020	91.7
Other education, training, and library workers..	101	76.0
Arts, design, entertainment, sports, and media occupations...............................	2,820	47.8
Artists and related workers..	213	48.6
Designers..	834	57.5
Actors..	30	-
Producers and directors..	154	38.5
Athletes, coaches, umpires, and related workers...	252	32.5
Dancers and choreographers..	25	-
Musicians, singers, and related workers..	186	29.3
Entertainers and performers, sports and related workers, all other.....................	39	-
Announcers...	41	-
News analysts, reporters and correspondents...	94	45.4
Public relations specialists..	135	61.6
Editors..	171	54.8

See note at end of table.

Occupation	Total employed	Percent women
Technical writers	47	-
Writers and authors	186	57.3
Miscellaneous media and communication workers	83	72.2
Broadcast and sound engineering technicians and radio operators	98	16.1
Photographers	181	44.1
Television, video, and motion picture camera operators and editors	50	15.3
Media and communication equipment workers, all other	1	-
Healthcare practitioner and technical occupations	7,399	74.6
Chiropractors	60	15.3
Dentists	152	27.2
Dietitians and nutritionists	100	90.0
Optometrists	37	-
Pharmacists	243	51.8
Physicians and surgeons	877	30.5
Physician assistants	99	66.9
Podiatrists	12	-
Registered nurses	2,778	91.7
Audiologists	12	-
Occupational therapists	87	95.9
Physical therapists	197	69.0
Radiation therapists	20	-
Recreational therapists	17	-
Respiratory therapists	109	68.3
Speech-language pathologists	133	98.1
Therapists, all other	107	80.8
Veterinarians	56	56.7
Health diagnosing and treating practitioners, all other	20	-
Clinical laboratory technologists and technicians	351	75.7
Dental hygienists	143	97.7
Diagnostic related technologists and technicians	298	72.0
Emergency medical technicians and paramedics	138	30.2
Health diagnosing and treating practitioner support technicians	447	76.7
Licensed practical and licensed vocational nurses	566	93.3
Medical records and health information technicians	98	95.0
Opticians, dispensing	50	63.4
Miscellaneous health technologists and technicians	139	63.0
Other healthcare practitioners and technical occupations	52	42.1
Service occupations	24,451	57.2
Healthcare support occupations	3,212	88.8
Nursing, psychiatric, and home health aides	1,889	88.7
Occupational therapist assistants and aides	7	-
Physical therapist assistants and aides	75	77.0
Massage therapists	147	84.5
Dental assistants	263	96.3
Medical assistants and other healthcare support occupations	831	88.8
Protective service occupations	3,047	22.8
First-line supervisors/managers of correctional officers	42	-
First-line supervisors/managers of police and detectives	117	14.7
First-line supervisors/managers of fire fighting and prevention workers	54	8.7
Supervisors, protective service workers, all other	102	21.7
Fire fighters	293	4.8

See note at end of table.

Table 11. **Employed persons by detailed occupation and sex, 2008 annual averages—Continued**

(Numbers in thousands)

Occupation	Total employed	Percent women
Fire inspectors	27	-
Bailiffs, correctional officers, and jailers	403	30.0
Detectives and criminal investigators	139	19.2
Fish and game wardens	4	-
Parking enforcement workers	6	-
Police and sheriff's patrol officers	674	14.7
Transit and railroad police	5	-
Animal control workers	9	-
Private detectives and investigators	89	39.4
Security guards and gaming surveillance officers	867	23.6
Crossing guards	68	73.5
Lifeguards and other protective service workers	148	52.3
Food preparation and serving related occupations	7,824	56.0
Chefs and head cooks	351	17.0
First-line supervisors/managers of food preparation and serving workers	635	57.8
Cooks	1,997	40.1
Food preparation workers	724	60.7
Bartenders	365	58.3
Combined food preparation and serving workers, including fast food	323	68.5
Counter attendants, cafeteria, food concession, and coffee shop	323	64.1
Waiters and waitresses	2,010	73.2
Food servers, nonrestaurant	187	70.5
Dining room and cafeteria attendants and bartender helpers	349	47.8
Dishwashers	289	22.7
Hosts and hostesses, restaurant, lounge, and coffee shop	263	88.7
Food preparation and serving related workers, all other	7	-
Building and grounds cleaning and maintenance occupations	5,445	40.2
First-line supervisors/managers of housekeeping and janitorial workers	296	39.9
First-line supervisors/managers of landscaping, lawn service, and groundskeeping workers	258	7.5
Janitors and building cleaners	2,125	32.2
Maids and housekeeping cleaners	1,434	89.8
Pest control workers	71	8.2
Grounds maintenance workers	1,262	6.1
Personal care and service occupations	4,923	78.4
First-line supervisors/managers of gaming workers	155	38.6
First-line supervisors/managers of personal service workers	174	73.2
Animal trainers	40	-
Nonfarm animal caretakers	157	73.5
Gaming services workers	111	51.5
Motion picture projectionists	7	-
Ushers, lobby attendants, and ticket takers	42	-
Miscellaneous entertainment attendants and related workers	166	43.0
Funeral service workers	13	-
Barbers	87	20.8
Hairdressers, hairstylists, and cosmetologists	773	90.6
Miscellaneous personal appearance workers	229	82.3
Baggage porters, bellhops, and concierges	72	17.3
Tour and travel guides	35	-
Transportation attendants	139	71.0
Child care workers	1,314	95.6
Personal and home care aides	871	85.4

See note at end of table.

Table 11. **Employed persons by detailed occupation and sex, 2008 annual averages—Continued**

(Numbers in thousands)

Occupation	Total employed	Percent women
Recreation and fitness workers	353	68.1
Residential advisors	70	65.8
Personal care and service workers, all other	114	54.1
Sales and office occupations	35,544	63.2
Sales and related occupations	16,295	49.5
First-line supervisors/managers of retail sales workers	3,471	43.3
First-line supervisors/managers of non-retail sales workers	1,287	26.1
Cashiers	3,031	75.5
Counter and rental clerks	161	50.4
Parts salespersons	119	10.8
Retail salespersons	3,416	52.2
Advertising sales agents	216	54.7
Insurance sales agents	573	46.9
Securities, commodities, and financial services sales agents	388	27.9
Travel agents	98	71.6
Sales representatives, services, all other	521	34.4
Sales representatives, wholesale and manufacturing	1,343	27.3
Models, demonstrators, and product promoters	74	79.0
Real estate brokers and sales agents	962	54.4
Sales engineers	40	-
Telemarketers	139	66.3
Door-to-door sales workers, news and street vendors, and related workers	243	62.2
Sales and related workers, all other	212	61.1
Office and administrative support occupations	19,249	74.8
First-line supervisors/managers of office and administrative support workers	1,641	71.2
Switchboard operators, including answering service	49	-
Telephone operators	48	-
Communications equipment operators, all other	11	-
Bill and account collectors	232	68.0
Billing and posting clerks and machine operators	516	90.9
Bookkeeping, accounting, and auditing clerks	1,434	91.5
Gaming cage workers	16	-
Payroll and timekeeping clerks	158	90.1
Procurement clerks	26	-
Tellers	466	84.8
Brokerage clerks	5	-
Correspondence clerks	7	-
Court, municipal, and license clerks	100	75.6
Credit authorizers, checkers, and clerks	64	71.1
Customer service representatives	1,908	68.3
Eligibility interviewers, government programs	63	83.9
File clerks	364	83.8
Hotel, motel, and resort desk clerks	120	71.9
Interviewers, except eligibility and loan	146	82.2
Library assistants, clerical	107	83.8
Loan interviewers and clerks	122	84.7
New accounts clerks	23	-
Order clerks	112	58.8
Human resources assistants, except payroll and timekeeping	52	84.8
Receptionists and information clerks	1,413	93.6
Reservation and transportation ticket agents and travel clerks	136	60.9

See note at end of table.

33

Table 11. **Employed persons by detailed occupation and sex, 2008 annual averages—Continued**

(Numbers in thousands)

Occupation	Total employed	Percent women
Information and record clerks, all other..........	107	91.1
Cargo and freight agents..........	19	-
Couriers and messengers..........	261	17.4
Dispatchers..........	286	57.4
Meter readers, utilities..........	45	-
Postal service clerks..........	167	53.7
Postal service mail carriers..........	373	33.0
Postal service mail sorters, processors, and processing machine operators..........	90	42.7
Production, planning, and expediting clerks..........	269	58.2
Shipping, receiving, and traffic clerks..........	543	32.8
Stock clerks and order fillers..........	1,481	35.4
Weighers, measurers, checkers, and samplers, recordkeeping..........	63	44.7
Secretaries and administrative assistants..........	3,296	96.1
Computer operators..........	134	51.4
Data entry keyers..........	415	77.3
Word processors and typists..........	149	92.9
Desktop publishers..........	4	-
Insurance claims and policy processing clerks..........	275	83.4
Mail clerks and mail machine operators, except postal service..........	123	49.0
Office clerks, general..........	1,176	84.4
Office machine operators, except computer..........	43	-
Proofreaders and copy markers..........	13	-
Statistical assistants..........	19	-
Office and administrative support workers, all other..........	558	77.3
Natural resources, construction, and maintenance occupations..........	14,806	4.2
Farming, fishing, and forestry occupations..........	988	21.1
First-line supervisors/managers of farming, fishing, and forestry workers..........	48	-
Agricultural inspectors..........	24	-
Animal breeders..........	12	-
Graders and sorters, agricultural products..........	63	65.3
Miscellaneous agricultural workers..........	723	19.3
Fishers and related fishing workers..........	36	-
Hunters and trappers..........	1	-
Forest and conservation workers..........	8	-
Logging workers..........	73	1.0
Construction and extraction occupations..........	8,667	2.5
First-line supervisors/managers of construction trades and extraction workers..........	844	2.7
Boilermakers..........	22	-
Brickmasons, blockmasons, and stonemasons..........	230	.4
Carpenters..........	1,562	1.5
Carpet, floor, and tile installers and finishers..........	224	2.3
Cement masons, concrete finishers, and terrazzo workers..........	90	-
Construction laborers..........	1,651	3.1
Paving, surfacing, and tamping equipment operators..........	24	-
Pile-driver operators..........	3	-
Operating engineers and other construction equipment operators..........	398	1.5
Drywall installers, ceiling tile installers, and tapers..........	209	2.1
Electricians..........	874	1.0
Glaziers..........	49	-
Insulation workers..........	38	-
Painters, construction and maintenance..........	647	6.3

See note at end of table.

Table 11. **Employed persons by detailed occupation and sex, 2008 annual averages—Continued**

(Numbers in thousands)

Occupation	Total employed	Percent women
Paperhangers..	8	-
Pipelayers, plumbers, pipefitters, and steamfitters...............................	606	1.4
Plasterers and stucco masons..	46	-
Reinforcing iron and rebar workers...	15	-
Roofers..	234	1.3
Sheet metal workers..	136	4.8
Structural iron and steel workers..	77	.9
Helpers, construction trades..	113	4.1
Construction and building inspectors..	93	9.5
Elevator installers and repairers..	38	-
Fence erectors...	38	-
Hazardous materials removal workers..	23	-
Highway maintenance workers..	103	1.9
Rail-track laying and maintenance equipment operators........................	15	-
Septic tank servicers and sewer pipe cleaners....................................	11	-
Miscellaneous construction and related workers..................................	38	-
Derrick, rotary drill, and service unit operators, oil, gas, and mining......	40	-
Earth drillers, except oil and gas..	35	-
Explosives workers, ordnance handling experts, and blasters................	11	-
Mining machine operators..	51	2.2
Roof bolters, mining..	4	-
Roustabouts, oil and gas...	7	-
Helpers—extraction workers..	7	-
Other extraction workers...	55	2.8
Installation, maintenance, and repair occupations................................	5,152	3.9
First-line supervisors/managers of mechanics, installers, and repairers..	300	8.0
Computer, automated teller, and office machine repairers.....................	335	10.5
Radio and telecommunications equipment installers and repairers..........	200	11.4
Avionics technicians..	18	-
Electric motor, power tool, and related repairers..................................	24	-
Electrical and electronics installers and repairers, transportation equipment....................	3	-
Electrical and electronics repairers, industrial and utility......................	18	-
Electronic equipment installers and repairers, motor vehicles................	27	-
Electronic home entertainment equipment installers and repairers..........	75	1.6
Security and fire alarm systems installers...	62	-
Aircraft mechanics and service technicians...	153	1.7
Automotive body and related repairers..	157	2.1
Automotive glass installers and repairers..	28	-
Automotive service technicians and mechanics....................................	852	1.6
Bus and truck mechanics and diesel engine specialists........................	358	.9
Heavy vehicle and mobile equipment service technicians and mechanics...	217	1.1
Small engine mechanics..	64	2.0
Miscellaneous vehicle and mobile equipment mechanics, installers, and repairers..............	86	1.9
Control and valve installers and repairers...	21	-
Heating, air conditioning, and refrigeration mechanics and installers.......	397	2.0
Home appliance repairers..	51	5.3
Industrial and refractory machinery mechanics....................................	439	2.6
Maintenance and repair workers, general..	461	3.5
Maintenance workers, machinery..	39	-
Millwrights...	60	.9
Electrical power-line installers and repairers.......................................	109	1.4

See note at end of table.

35

Occupation	Total employed	Percent women
Telecommunications line installers and repairers..	204	3.3
Precision instrument and equipment repairers..	58	15.4
Coin, vending, and amusement machine servicers and repairers..............................	41	-
Commercial divers..	3	-
Locksmiths and safe repairers...	31	-
Manufactured building and mobile home installers...	12	-
Riggers..	8	-
Signal and track switch repairers...	5	-
Helpers—installation, maintenance, and repair workers...	23	-
Other installation, maintenance, and repair workers...	213	7.5
Production, transportation, and material moving occupations...............................	17,800	22.4
Production occupations...	8,973	29.7
First-line supervisors/managers of production and operating workers........................	874	18.1
Aircraft structure, surfaces, rigging, and systems assemblers...................................	18	-
Electrical, electronics, and electromechanical assemblers..	203	57.8
Engine and other machine assemblers...	13	-
Structural metal fabricators and fitters...	36	-
Miscellaneous assemblers and fabricators...	1,050	35.0
Bakers..	194	55.7
Butchers and other meat, poultry, and fish processing workers.................................	309	26.8
Food and tobacco roasting, baking, and drying machine operators and tenders.........	11	-
Food batchmakers...	73	53.5
Food cooking machine operators and tenders...	7	-
Computer control programmers and operators...	68	8.7
Extruding and drawing machine setters, operators, and tenders, metal and plastic.....	9	-
Forging machine setters, operators, and tenders, metal and plastic...........................	9	-
Rolling machine setters, operators, and tenders, metal and plastic............................	12	-
Cutting, punching, and press machine setters, operators, and tenders, metal and plastic.......	105	20.2
Drilling and boring machine tool setters, operators, and tenders, metal and plastic.....	4	-
Grinding, lapping, polishing, and buffing machine tool setters, operators, and tenders, metal and plastic........................	50	19.7
Lathe and turning machine tool setters, operators, and tenders, metal and plastic......	20	-
Milling and planing machine setters, operators, and tenders, metal and plastic..........	8	-
Machinists..	409	6.9
Metal furnace and kiln operators and tenders...	24	-
Model makers and patternmakers, metal and plastic...	10	-
Molders and molding machine setters, operators, and tenders, metal and plastic.......	58	18.1
Multiple machine tool setters, operators, and tenders, metal and plastic....................	4	-
Tool and die makers...	71	1.0
Welding, soldering, and brazing workers..	598	4.7
Heat treating equipment setters, operators, and tenders, metal and plastic...............	11	-
Lay-out workers, metal and plastic...	9	-
Plating and coating machine setters, operators, and tenders, metal and plastic.........	13	-
Tool grinders, filers, and sharpeners...	7	-
Metalworkers and plastic workers, all other..	349	21.1
Bookbinders and bindery workers...	36	-
Job printers..	47	-
Prepress technicians and workers..	44	-
Printing machine operators...	213	19.8
Laundry and dry-cleaning workers..	239	60.8
Pressers, textile, garment, and related materials..	57	79.2

See note at end of table.

(Numbers in thousands)

Occupation	Total employed	Percent women
Sewing machine operators	226	78.2
Shoe and leather workers and repairers	8	-
Shoe machine operators and tenders	6	-
Tailors, dressmakers, and sewers	71	84.2
Textile bleaching and dyeing machine operators and tenders	3	-
Textile cutting machine setters, operators, and tenders	6	-
Textile knitting and weaving machine setters, operators, and tenders	5	-
Textile winding, twisting, and drawing out machine setters, operators, and tenders	17	-
Extruding, forming, pressing, and compacting machine setters, operators, and tenders	2	-
Fabric and apparel patternmakers	2	-
Upholsterers	56	19.7
Textile, apparel, and furnishings workers, all other	21	-
Cabinetmakers and bench carpenters	85	6.5
Furniture finishers	19	-
Sawing machine setters, operators, and tenders, wood	44	-
Woodworking machine setters, operators, and tenders, except sawing	22	-
Woodworkers, all other	37	-
Power plant operators, distributors, and dispatchers	55	9.2
Stationary engineers and boiler operators	101	1.7
Water and liquid waste treatment plant and system operators	71	8.6
Miscellaneous plant and system operators	34	-
Chemical processing machine setters, operators, and tenders	52	15.4
Crushing, grinding, polishing, mixing, and blending workers	108	13.3
Cutting workers	80	26.7
Extruding, forming, pressing, and compacting machine setters, operators, and tenders	29	-
Furnace, kiln, oven, drier, and kettle operators and tenders	16	-
Inspectors, testers, sorters, samplers, and weighers	751	41.3
Jewelers and precious stone and metal workers	59	47.0
Medical, dental, and ophthalmic laboratory technicians	95	56.9
Packaging and filling machine operators and tenders	261	51.5
Painting workers	183	13.6
Photographic process workers and processing machine operators	53	47.8
Semiconductor processors	7	-
Cementing and gluing machine operators and tenders	11	-
Cleaning, washing, and metal pickling equipment operators and tenders	10	-
Cooling and freezing equipment operators and tenders	2	-
Etchers and engravers	7	-
Molders, shapers, and casters, except metal and plastic	38	-
Paper goods machine setters, operators, and tenders	42	-
Tire builders	14	-
Helpers—production workers	34	-
Production workers, all other	958	31.0
Transportation and material moving occupations	8,827	14.9
Supervisors, transportation and material moving workers	208	20.5
Aircraft pilots and flight engineers	141	2.6
Air traffic controllers and airfield operations specialists	27	-
Ambulance drivers and attendants, except emergency medical technicians	16	-
Bus drivers	651	49.0
Driver/sales workers and truck drivers	3,388	4.9
Taxi drivers and chauffeurs	373	13.3
Motor vehicle operators, all other	66	18.0

See note at end of table.

Table 11. **Employed persons by detailed occupation and sex, 2008 annual averages—Continued**

(Numbers in thousands)

Occupation	Total employed	Percent women
Locomotive engineers and operators..	58	2.8
Railroad brake, signal, and switch operators..	5	-
Railroad conductors and yardmasters..	53	4.7
Subway, streetcar, and other rail transportation workers............................	18	-
Sailors and marine oilers..	18	-
Ship and boat captains and operators..	39	-
Ship engineers..	5	-
Bridge and lock tenders..	7	-
Parking lot attendants...	83	12.6
Service station attendants...	87	14.8
Transportation inspectors..	51	11.3
Other transportation workers..	19	-
Conveyor operators and tenders...	5	-
Crane and tower operators..	69	3.7
Dredge, excavating, and loading machine operators....................................	60	1.2
Hoist and winch operators...	5	-
Industrial truck and tractor operators...	568	8.9
Cleaners of vehicles and equipment...	317	9.5
Laborers and freight, stock, and material movers, hand...............................	1,889	17.1
Machine feeders and offbearers...	34	-
Packers and packagers, hand...	391	58.1
Pumping station operators..	25	-
Refuse and recyclable material collectors..	98	14.0
Shuttle car operators..	5	-
Tank car, truck, and ship loaders...	2	-
Material moving workers, all other...	48	-

NOTE: Dash indicates data not shown for occupations where employment base is less than 50,000.

SOURCE: Current Population Survey, U.S. Department of Labor, U.S. Bureau of Labor Statistics.

Table 12. **Employed women by occupation, race, and Hispanic or Latino ethnicity, 2008 annual averages**

(Percent distribution)

Occupation	White	Black or African American	Asian	Hispanic or Latino ethnicity
Total, 16 years and over (thousands)............................	54,501	8,554	3,225	8,098
Percent..	100.0	100.0	100.0	100.0
Management, professional, and related occupations	40.6	31.3	46.0	23.5
Management, business, and financial operations occupations ...	14.3	10.4	16.4	8.8
Professional and related occupations	26.3	20.9	29.7	14.7
Service occupations	19.3	28.2	19.4	31.3
Sales and office occupations	33.7	31.9	26.1	32.9
Sales and related occupations	12.0	11.1	11.4	12.1
Office and administrative support occupations	21.7	20.7	14.7	20.7
Natural resources, construction, and maintenance occupations	.9	.7	.6	1.7
Farming, fishing, and forestry occupations	.3	.1	.2	.9
Construction and extraction occupations	.3	.3	.1	.4
Installation, maintenance, and repair occupations	.3	.3	.3	.4
Production, transportation, and material moving occupations	5.4	7.9	7.8	10.6
Production occupations	3.6	4.8	6.6	7.4
Transportation and material moving occupations	1.8	3.1	1.2	3.2

SOURCE: Current Population Survey, U.S. Department of Labor, U.S. Bureau of Labor Statistics.

Table 13. Employed persons by industry and sex, 2007 and 2008 annual averages

(Numbers in thousands)

Industry and sex	Year			
	2007		2008	
	Number	Percent	Number	Percent
Total, both sexes				
Total, 16 years and over...	146,047	100.0	145,362	100.0
Agriculture, forestry, fishing, and hunting	2,095	1.4	2,168	1.5
Mining	736	.5	819	0.6
Construction	11,856	8.1	10,974	7.5
Manufacturing	16,302	11.2	15,904	10.9
Durable goods	10,363	7.1	10,273	7.1
Nondurable goods	5,938	4.1	5,631	3.9
Wholesale and retail trade	20,937	14.3	20,585	14.2
Wholesale trade	4,367	3.0	4,052	2.8
Retail trade	16,570	11.3	16,533	11.4
Transportation and utilities	7,650	5.2	7,727	5.3
Transportation and warehousing	6,457	4.4	6,501	4.5
Utilities	1,193	.8	1,225	0.8
Information	3,566	2.4	3,481	2.4
Financial activities	10,488	7.2	10,228	7.0
Finance and insurance	7,306	5.0	7,279	5.0
Real estate and rental and leasing	3,182	2.2	2,949	2.0
Professional and business services	15,621	10.7	15,540	10.7
Professional and technical services	9,208	6.3	9,362	6.4
Management, administrative, and waste services...................	6,412	4.4	6,178	4.3
Education and health services	30,662	21.0	31,402	21.6
Educational services	12,828	8.8	13,169	9.1
Health care and social assistance	17,834	12.2	18,233	12.5
Hospitals	5,955	4.1	6,241	4.3
Health services, except hospitals	8,733	6.0	8,865	6.1
Social assistance	3,147	2.2	3,127	2.2
Leisure and hospitality	12,415	8.5	12,767	8.8
Arts, entertainment, and recreation	2,833	1.9	2,972	2.0
Accommodation and food services	9,582	6.6	9,795	6.7
Other services	6,972	4.8	7,005	4.8
Other services, except private households	6,159	4.2	6,200	4.3
Private households	813	.6	805	0.6
Public administration	6,746	4.6	6,763	4.7

Table 13. **Employed persons by industry and sex, 2007 and 2008 annual averages—Continued**

(Numbers in thousands)

Industry and sex	Year			
	2007		2008	
	Number	Percent	Number	Percent
Women				
Total, 16 years and over...	67,792	100.0	67,876	100.0
Agriculture, forestry, fishing, and hunting	490	.7	518	.8
Mining	101	.1	105	.2
Construction	1,119	1.7	1,069	1.6
Manufacturing	4,885	7.2	4,655	6.9
Durable goods	2,696	4.0	2,624	3.9
Nondurable goods	2,189	3.2	2,030	3.0
Wholesale and retail trade	9,414	13.9	9,257	13.6
Wholesale trade	1,276	1.9	1,196	1.8
Retail trade	8,138	12.0	8,062	11.9
Transportation and utilities	1,878	2.8	1,786	2.6
Transportation and warehousing	1,621	2.4	1,547	2.3
Utilities	257	.4	239	.4
Information	1,501	2.2	1,449	2.1
Financial activities	5,807	8.6	5,605	8.3
Finance and insurance	4,276	6.3	4,223	6.2
Real estate and rental and leasing	1,531	2.3	1,382	2.0
Professional and business services	6,659	9.8	6,584	9.7
Professional and technical services	4,040	6.0	4,130	6.1
Management, administrative, and waste services.................	2,619	3.9	2,453	3.6
Education and health services	22,906	33.8	23,603	34.8
Educational services	8,866	13.1	9,174	13.5
Health care and social assistance	14,040	20.7	14,429	21.3
Hospitals	4,491	6.6	4,790	7.1
Health services, except hospitals	6,880	10.1	6,965	10.3
Social assistance	2,669	3.9	2,674	3.9
Leisure and hospitality	6,377	9.4	6,575	9.7
Arts, entertainment, and recreation	1,320	1.9	1,372	2.0
Accommodation and food services	5,057	7.5	5,203	7.7
Other services	3,628	5.4	3,615	5.3
Other services, except private households	2,892	4.3	2,881	4.2
Private households	737	1.1	735	1.1
Public administration	3,026	4.5	3,056	4.5

41

Table 13. **Employed persons by industry and sex, 2007 and 2008 annual averages—Continued**

(Numbers in thousands)

Industry and sex	Year			
	2007		2008	
	Number	Percent	Number	Percent
Men				
Total, 16 years and over..	78,254	100.0	77,486	100.0
Agriculture, forestry, fishing, and hunting	1,604	2.0	1,650	2.1
Mining	635	.8	714	.9
Construction	10,738	13.7	9,905	12.8
Manufacturing	11,416	14.6	11,249	14.5
Durable goods	7,667	9.8	7,649	9.9
Nondurable goods	3,749	4.8	3,601	4.6
Wholesale and retail trade	11,523	14.7	11,327	14.6
Wholesale trade	3,091	3.9	2,856	3.7
Retail trade	8,433	10.8	8,471	10.9
Transportation and utilities	5,772	7.4	5,940	7.7
Transportation and warehousing	4,836	6.2	4,954	6.4
Utilities	936	1.2	987	1.3
Information	2,065	2.6	2,032	2.6
Financial activities	4,681	6.0	4,623	6.0
Finance and insurance	3,030	3.9	3,056	3.9
Real estate and rental and leasing	1,651	2.1	1,567	2.0
Professional and business services	8,962	11.5	8,957	11.6
Professional and technical services	5,168	6.6	5,232	6.8
Management, administrative, and waste services.................	3,794	4.8	3,725	4.8
Education and health services	7,756	9.9	7,799	10.1
Educational services	3,962	5.1	3,994	5.2
Health care and social assistance	3,794	4.8	3,805	4.9
Hospitals	1,464	1.9	1,451	1.9
Health services, except hospitals	1,852	2.4	1,900	2.5
Social assistance	478	.6	453	.6
Leisure and hospitality	6,038	7.7	6,192	8.0
Arts, entertainment, and recreation	1,514	1.9	1,600	2.1
Accommodation and food services	4,525	5.8	4,592	5.9
Other services	3,343	4.3	3,390	4.4
Other services, except private households	3,267	4.2	3,319	4.3
Private households	76	.1	70	.1
Public administration	3,720	4.8	3,707	4.8

SOURCE: Current Population Survey, U.S. Department of Labor, U.S. Bureau of Labor Statistics.

Table 14. Employed persons by detailed industry and sex, 2008 annual averages

(Numbers in thousands)

Industry	Total employed	Percent women
Total, 16 years and over..	145,362	46.7
Agriculture, forestry, fishing, and hunting...	2,168	23.9
Crop production...	954	22.3
Animal production..	864	25.5
Forestry, except logging..	59	35.2
Logging...	86	4.4
Fishing, hunting, and trapping...	53	11.7
Support activities for agriculture and forestry...	152	35.8
Mining..	819	12.9
Oil and gas extraction...	76	17.5
Coal mining...	100	7.2
Metal ore mining..	36	-
Nonmetallic mineral mining and quarrying...	101	14.4
Not specified type of mining..	7	-
Support activities for mining..	498	13.0
Construction...	10,974	9.7
Manufacturing..	15,904	29.3
Durable goods...	10,273	25.5
Nonmetallic mineral products...	521	17.8
Pottery, ceramics, and related product manufacturing............................	24	-
Structural clay product manufacturing...	45	-
Glass and glass products...	162	27.7
Cement, concrete, lime, and gypsum products..	205	7.5
Miscellaneous nonmetallic mineral product manufacturing.....................	85	16.4
Primary metals and fabricated metal products...	1,798	16.9
Iron and steel mills and steel products..	317	12.3
Aluminum production and processing...	75	13.1
Nonferrous metal, except aluminum, production and processing.............	62	20.6
Foundries..	80	13.6
Metal forgings and stampings..	49	-
Cutlery and hand tools...	47	-
Structural metals and tanks and shipping containers.............................	403	15.9
Machine shops; turned products; screws, nuts, and bolts.......................	300	13.9
Coating, engraving, heat treating and allied activities............................	85	17.1
Ordnance..	38	-
Miscellaneous fabricated metal product manufacturing...........................	332	23.4
Not specified metal industries..	9	-
Machinery manufacturing..	1,308	22.2
Agricultural implements..	107	19.8
Construction, mining, and oil field machinery..	149	16.3
Commercial and service industry machinery..	107	38.6
Metalworking machinery...	166	17.9
Engines, turbines, and power transmission equipment............................	60	29.0
Machinery manufacturing, n.e.c.	706	22.0
Not specified machinery manufacturing...	12	-
Computers and electronic products..	1,467	32.7
Computer and peripheral equipment..	345	28.8
Communications, audio, and video equipment..	190	31.2
Navigational, measuring, electromedical, and control instruments.........	214	32.8
Electronic component and product manufacturing, n.e.c.	718	35.0

See note at end of table.

(Numbers in thousands)

Industry	Total employed	Percent women
Electrical equipment and appliances...	492	32.8
Household appliances...	84	32.2
Electrical lighting, equipment, and supplies manufacturing, n.e.c........................	408	32.9
Transportation equipment...	2,333	22.8
Motor vehicles and motor vehicle equipment.......................................	1,241	25.1
Aircraft and parts..	432	21.8
Aerospace products and parts...	428	20.7
Railroad rolling stock manufacturing...	21	-
Ship and boat building..	166	16.4
Other transportation equipment manufacturing..................................	45	-
Wood products..	481	19.0
Sawmills and wood preservation..	132	11.2
Veneer, plywood, and engineered wood products.............................	48	-
Prefabricated wood buildings and mobile homes...............................	48	-
Miscellaneous wood products..	253	23.7
Furniture and related products manufacturing..................................	582	28.1
Miscellaneous manufacturing...	1,291	39.3
Medical equipment and supplies manufacturing................................	547	42.5
Toys, amusement, and sporting goods manufacturing.......................	147	32.1
Miscellaneous manufacturing, n.e.c...	428	37.6
Not specified manufacturing industries...	169	39.7
Nondurable goods..	5,631	36.1
Food manufacturing...	1,575	37.0
Animal food, grain, and oilseed milling...	148	26.3
Sugar and confectionery products..	82	45.6
Fruit and vegetable preserving and specialty foods...........................	171	31.5
Dairy products..	138	26.2
Animal slaughtering and processing..	488	35.4
Retail bakeries...	151	63.0
Bakeries, except retail...	209	38.0
Seafood and other miscellaneous foods, n.e.c..................................	171	38.3
Not specified food industries..	17	-
Beverages and tobacco products...	257	27.2
Beverages manufacturing..	230	25.6
Tobacco manufacturing...	27	-
Textiles, apparel, and leather..	700	55.5
Fiber, yarn, and thread mills...	18	-
Fabric mills, except knitting..	136	42.5
Textile and fabric finishing and coating mills...................................	19	-
Carpet and rug mills..	51	38.3
Textile product mills, except carpets and rugs..................................	92	51.2
Knitting mills..	15	-
Cut and sew apparel..	293	63.7
Apparel accessories and other apparel manufacturing.......................	10	-
Footwear manufacturing...	39	-
Leather tanning and products, except footwear manufacturing.............	27	-
Paper and printing..	1,087	32.5
Pulp, paper, and paperboard mills..	214	21.5
Paperboard containers and boxes...	118	27.9
Miscellaneous paper and pulp products...	77	35.9
Printing and related support activities...	678	36.4
Petroleum and coal products...	169	21.1
Petroleum refining...	145	21.6

See note at end of table.

Industry	Total employed	Percent women
Miscellaneous petroleum and coal products	24	-
Chemicals	1,293	34.7
Resins, synthetic rubber and fibers, and filaments	165	29.6
Agricultural chemical manufacturing	28	-
Pharmaceuticals and medicines	457	46.4
Paints, coatings, and adhesives	71	19.0
Soaps, cleaning compounds, and cosmetics	146	51.6
Industrial and miscellaneous chemicals	425	22.5
Plastics and rubber products	550	27.5
Plastics product manufacturing	389	28.8
Tire manufacturing	70	14.4
Rubber product, except tire, manufacturing	92	31.9
Wholesale and retail trade	20,585	45.0
Wholesale trade	4,052	29.5
Motor vehicles, parts and supplies, merchant wholesalers	216	27.6
Furniture and home furnishings, merchant wholesalers	90	40.0
Lumber and other construction materials, merchant wholesalers	230	21.0
Professional and commercial equipment and supplies, merchant wholesalers	351	37.4
Metals and minerals, except petroleum, merchant wholesalers	66	22.7
Electrical goods, merchant wholesalers	224	26.4
Hardware, plumbing and heating equipment, and supplies, merchant wholesalers	172	28.4
Machinery, equipment, and supplies, merchant wholesalers	424	25.1
Recyclable materials, merchant wholesalers	122	10.1
Miscellaneous durable goods, merchant wholesalers	123	38.2
Paper and paper products, merchant wholesalers	82	46.0
Drugs, sundries, and chemical and allied products, merchant wholesalers	255	40.2
Apparel, fabrics, and notions, merchant wholesalers	128	44.0
Groceries and related products, merchant wholesalers	829	23.7
Farm product raw materials, merchant wholesalers	68	23.8
Petroleum and petroleum products, merchant wholesalers	144	33.9
Alcoholic beverages, merchant wholesalers	149	17.0
Farm supplies, merchant wholesalers	37	-
Miscellaneous nondurable goods, merchant wholesalers	198	41.2
Wholesale electronic markets, agents and brokers	74	47.3
Not specified wholesale trade	70	36.2
Retail trade	16,533	48.8
Automobile dealers	1,350	19.8
Other motor vehicle dealers	175	21.5
Auto parts, accessories, and tire stores	507	16.9
Furniture and home furnishings stores	655	42.5
Household appliance stores	85	30.9
Radio, TV, and computer stores	629	31.7
Building material and supplies dealers	960	28.2
Hardware stores	222	32.9
Lawn and garden equipment and supplies stores	279	31.8
Grocery stores	2,644	50.0
Specialty food stores	254	43.9
Beer, wine, and liquor stores	144	34.2
Pharmacies and drug stores	859	64.8
Health and personal care, except drug, stores	320	65.2
Gasoline stations	507	50.2
Clothing and accessories, except shoe, stores	965	74.9

See note at end of table.

Table 14. **Employed persons by detailed industry and sex, 2008 annual averages—Continued**

(Numbers in thousands)

Industry	Total employed	Percent women
Shoe stores	137	60.3
Jewelry, luggage, and leather goods stores	247	65.7
Sporting goods, camera, and hobby and toy stores	470	44.5
Sewing, needlework, and piece goods stores	76	74.7
Music stores	80	36.5
Book stores and news dealers	190	65.3
Department stores and discount stores	2,298	61.9
Miscellaneous general merchandise stores	491	56.1
Retail florists	145	73.4
Office supplies and stationery stores	163	38.1
Used merchandise stores	195	62.0
Gift, novelty, and souvenir shops	189	80.0
Miscellaneous retail stores	412	57.5
Electronic shopping	92	47.8
Electronic auctions	27	-
Mail order houses	96	65.5
Vending machine operators	62	22.1
Fuel dealers	114	24.6
Other direct selling establishments	230	70.0
Not specified retail trade	263	56.4
Transportation and utilities	7,727	23.1
Transportation and warehousing	6,501	23.8
Air transportation	569	34.6
Rail transportation	284	5.9
Water transportation	76	30.9
Truck transportation	1,994	14.0
Bus service and urban transit	574	38.9
Taxi and limousine service	275	11.6
Pipeline transportation	35	-
Scenic and sightseeing transportation	34	-
Services incidental to transportation	733	26.5
Postal Service	831	39.3
Couriers and messengers	710	19.9
Warehousing and storage	385	25.1
Utilities	1,225	19.5
Electric power generation, transmission, and distribution	622	17.9
Natural gas distribution	126	20.1
Electric and gas, and other combinations	84	26.4
Water, steam, air-conditioning, and irrigation systems	259	20.9
Sewage treatment facilities	108	15.5
Not specified utilities	26	-
Information	3,481	41.6
Newspaper publishers	407	45.8
Publishing, except newspapers and software	303	55.2
Software publishing	79	41.1
Motion pictures and video industries	397	33.0
Sound recording industries	41	-
Radio and television broadcasting and cable	578	33.4
Internet publishing and broadcasting	34	-
Wired telecommunications carriers	971	35.4
Other telecommunications services	234	42.9

See note at end of table.

Table 14. **Employed persons by detailed industry and sex, 2008 annual averages—Continued**

(Numbers in thousands)

Industry	Total employed	Percent women
Internet service providers..	78	32.0
Data processing, hosting, and related services...................	87	51.9
Libraries and archives...	218	81.5
Other information services...	55	49.6
Financial activities..	10,228	54.8
Finance and insurance...	7,279	58.0
Banking and related activities...	2,133	65.4
Savings institutions, including credit unions.......................	290	74.7
Non-depository credit and related activities.......................	949	52.7
Securities, commodities, funds, trusts, and other financial investments....	1,359	39.2
Insurance carriers and related activities............................	2,548	62.0
Real estate and rental and leasing..	2,949	46.9
Real estate..	2,475	50.0
Rental and leasing services...	474	30.5
Automotive equipment rental and leasing...........................	183	31.1
Videotape and disk rental...	78	46.6
Other consumer goods rental...	86	28.4
Commercial, industrial, and other intangible assets rental and leasing..............	127	21.3
Professional and business services..	15,540	42.4
Professional and technical services...................................	9,362	44.1
Legal services..	1,642	58.6
Accounting, tax preparation, bookkeeping, and payroll services...........................	1,002	62.8
Architectural, engineering, and related services.................	1,615	25.8
Specialized design services..	386	59.7
Computer systems design and related services..................	1,945	25.5
Management, scientific, and technical consulting services....	1,112	43.4
Scientific research and development services.....................	543	47.4
Advertising and related services.......................................	520	49.9
Veterinary services..	246	81.7
Other professional, scientific, and technical services..........	352	55.5
Management, administrative, and waste services....................	6,178	39.7
Management of companies and enterprises.........................	67	60.7
Employment services...	984	58.5
Business support services..	801	62.9
Travel arrangement and reservation services.....................	272	61.6
Investigation and security services....................................	814	26.6
Services to buildings and dwellings...................................	1,350	50.1
Landscaping services...	1,229	8.6
Other administrative and other support services.................	226	45.3
Waste management and remediation services.....................	437	15.1
Education and health services...	31,402	75.2
Educational services..	13,169	69.7
Elementary and secondary schools....................................	9,036	75.6
Colleges and universities, including junior colleges.............	3,361	53.8
Business, technical, and trade schools and training............	100	55.2
Other schools, instruction, and educational services...........	671	71.2
Health care and social assistance.....................................	18,233	79.1
Hospitals...	6,241	76.7

See note at end of table.

47

(Numbers in thousands)

Industry	Total employed	Percent women
Health services, except hospitals...	8,865	78.6
Offices of physicians...	1,562	76.0
Offices of dentists...	774	82.4
Offices of chiropractors..	139	58.3
Offices of optometrists...	110	78.0
Offices of other health practitioners..	195	73.4
Outpatient care centers..	1,107	76.0
Home health care services...	881	89.1
Other health care services..	1,647	71.4
Nursing care facilities...	1,779	87.0
Residential care facilities, without nursing..	673	71.4
Social assistance..	3,127	85.5
Individual and family services...	1,284	78.0
Community food and housing, and emergency services......................	111	65.6
Vocational rehabilitation services...	169	64.6
Child day care services..	1,563	95.3
Leisure and hospitality..	12,767	51.5
Arts, entertainment, and recreation..	2,972	46.2
Independent artists, performing arts, spectator sports, and related industries........	810	43.2
Museums, art galleries, historical sites, and similar institutions............	379	45.3
Bowling centers...	52	45.9
Other amusement, gambling, and recreation industries.......................	1,730	47.8
Accommodation and food services..	9,795	53.1
Accommodation...	1,523	56.9
Traveler accommodation..	1,423	57.4
Recreational vehicle parks and camps, and rooming and boarding houses........	100	50.6
Food services and drinking places...	8,272	52.4
Restaurants and other food services...	8,032	52.4
Drinking places, alcoholic beverages...	240	54.6
Other services..	7,005	51.6
Other services, except private households...	6,200	46.5
Repair and maintenance...	2,086	12.3
Automotive repair and maintenance...	1,208	10.6
Car washes..	175	14.7
Electronic and precision equipment repair and maintenance...............	177	14.8
Commercial and industrial machinery and equipment repair and maintenance....	320	6.9
Personal and household goods repair and maintenance.......................	199	26.4
Footwear and leather goods repair..	6	-
Personal and laundry services..	2,240	71.3
Barber shops...	95	25.2
Beauty salons..	929	90.0
Nail salons and other personal care services.......................................	365	75.1
Drycleaning and laundry services...	378	61.4
Funeral homes, cemeteries, and crematories.......................................	124	27.6
Other personal services..	348	56.6
Membership associations and organizations..	1,874	54.8
Religious organizations...	1,060	48.0
Civic, social, advocacy organizations, and grantmaking and giving services........	601	67.3
Labor unions...	59	49.4
Business, professional, political, and similar organizations.................	155	54.6
Private households..	805	91.3

See note at end of table.

Table 14. **Employed persons by detailed industry and sex, 2008 annual averages—Continued**

(Numbers in thousands)

Industry	Total employed	Percent women
Public administration...	6,763	45.2
Executive offices and legislative bodies...	890	54.8
Public finance activities...	350	67.1
Other general government and support..	162	35.5
Justice, public order, and safety activities...	2,858	35.9
Administration of human resource programs......................................	922	71.0
Administration of environmental quality and housing programs...........	319	39.4
Administration of economic programs and space research..................	558	41.2
National security and international affairs...	703	33.8

n.e.c. = not elsewhere classified.

NOTE: Dash indicates data not shown for industries where employment base is less than 50,000.

SOURCE: Current Population Survey, U.S. Department of Labor, U.S. Bureau of Labor Statistics.

Table 15. **Employed women by industry, race, and Hispanic or Latino ethnicity, 2008 annual averages**

(Percent distribution)

Industry	White	Black or African American	Asian	Hispanic or Latino ethnicity
Total, 16 years and over (thousands)......................	54,501	8,554	3,225	8,098
Percent..	100.0	100.0	100.0	100.0
Agriculture and related industries	0.9	0.1	0.3	1.0
Mining	.2	.1	.1	.1
Construction	1.7	.8	.7	1.3
Manufacturing	6.8	6.0	10.7	8.8
Durable goods	3.9	3.0	6.2	4.1
Nondurable goods	2.9	3.0	4.4	4.7
Wholesale and retail trade	14.0	11.5	12.7	14.7
Wholesale trade	1.9	1.1	2.1	2.0
Retail trade	12.1	10.4	10.5	12.6
Transportation and utilities	2.5	3.8	2.1	2.9
Transportation and warehousing	2.1	3.5	1.8	2.6
Utilities	.4	.4	.3	.3
Information	2.1	2.3	2.0	1.4
Financial activities	8.4	7.3	8.1	7.2
Finance and insurance	6.3	5.8	6.6	5.4
Real estate and rental and leasing	2.2	1.5	1.5	1.9
Professional and business services	9.9	8.1	10.4	10.0
Professional and technical services	6.4	3.6	8.3	3.8
Management, administrative, and waste services...........	3.5	4.6	2.1	6.2
Education and health services	34.3	40.5	30.9	28.7
Educational services	14.1	12.3	8.9	10.0
Health care and social assistance	20.2	28.2	22.0	18.7
Hospitals	6.7	8.3	9.8	4.6
Health services, except hospitals	9.8	13.7	9.4	9.4
Social assistance	3.6	6.2	2.8	4.7
Leisure and hospitality	9.6	8.4	11.1	13.0
Arts, entertainment, and recreation	2.1	1.3	2.0	1.6
Accommodation and food services	7.5	7.2	9.2	11.5
Other services	5.4	4.1	7.5	7.3
Other services, except private households	4.3	3.3	6.9	3.9
Private households	1.1	.9	.7	3.5
Public administration	4.1	7.0	3.5	3.6

SOURCE: Current Population Survey, U.S. Department of Labor, U.S. Bureau of Labor Statistics.

Table 16. **Median usual weekly earnings of full-time wage and salary workers in current dollars by race, Hispanic or Latino ethnicity, and sex, 1979-2008 annual averages**

Year	Total, both sexes					Women				
	Total	White	Black or African American	Asian	Hispanic or Latino ethnicity	Total	White	Black or African American	Asian	Hispanic or Latino ethnicity
1979.......	$241	$248	$199	-	$194	$182	$184	$169	-	$157
1980.......	262	269	212	-	209	201	203	185	-	172
1981.......	284	291	235	-	223	219	221	206	-	190
1982.......	302	310	245	-	240	239	242	217	-	203
1983.......	313	320	261	-	250	252	254	232	-	215
1984.......	326	336	269	-	259	265	268	241	-	223
1985.......	344	356	277	-	270	277	281	252	-	230
1986 [1].....	359	371	291	-	277	291	294	264	-	241
1987.......	374	384	301	-	285	303	307	276	-	251
1988.......	385	395	314	-	290	315	318	288	-	260
1989.......	399	409	319	-	298	328	334	301	-	269
1990 [1].....	412	424	329	-	304	346	353	308	-	278
1991.......	426	442	348	-	312	366	373	323	-	292
1992.......	440	458	357	-	321	380	387	335	-	302
1993.......	459	475	369	-	331	393	401	348	-	313
1994 [1].....	467	484	371	-	324	399	408	346	-	305
1995.......	479	494	383	-	329	406	415	355	-	305
1996.......	490	506	387	-	339	418	428	362	-	316
1997 [1].....	503	519	400	-	351	431	444	375	-	318
1998 [1].....	523	545	426	-	370	456	468	400	-	337
1999 [1].....	549	573	445	-	385	473	483	409	-	348
2000 [1].....	576	590	474	$615	399	493	502	429	$547	366
2001.......	596	610	491	639	417	512	522	454	563	388
2002.......	608	623	498	658	424	529	547	473	566	397
2003 [1].....	620	636	514	693	440	552	567	491	598	410
2004.......	638	657	525	708	456	573	584	505	613	419
2005......	651	672	520	753	471	585	596	499	665	429
2006	671	690	554	784	486	600	609	519	699	440
2007.......	695	716	569	830	503	614	626	533	731	473
2008 [1].....	722	742	589	861	529	638	654	554	753	501

See footnote at end of table.

Table 16. **Median usual weekly earnings of full-time wage and salary workers in current dollars by race, Hispanic or Latino ethnicity, and sex, 1979-2008 annual averages—Continued**

Year	Men					Women's earnings as a percent of men's				
	Total	White	Black or African American	Asian	Hispanic or Latino ethnicity	Total	White	Black or African American	Asian	Hispanic or Latino ethnicity
1979......	$292	$298	$227	-	$219	62.3	61.7	74.4	-	71.7
1980.......	313	320	244	-	234	64.2	63.4	75.8	-	73.5
1981.......	340	350	268	-	251	64.4	63.1	76.9	-	75.7
1982.......	364	375	278	-	269	65.7	64.5	78.1	-	75.5
1983.......	379	387	294	-	274	66.5	65.6	78.9	-	78.5
1984.......	392	401	303	-	287	67.6	66.8	79.5	-	77.7
1985.......	407	418	305	-	296	68.1	67.2	82.6	-	77.7
1986 [1].....	419	433	319	-	299	69.5	67.9	82.8	-	80.6
1987.......	434	450	327	-	306	69.8	68.2	84.4	-	82.0
1988.......	449	465	348	-	308	70.2	68.4	82.8	-	84.4
1989.......	468	482	348	-	315	70.1	69.3	86.5	-	85.4
1990 [1].....	481	494	361	-	318	71.9	71.5	85.3	-	87.4
1991.......	493	506	375	-	323	74.2	73.7	86.1	-	90.4
1992.......	501	514	380	-	339	75.8	75.3	88.2	-	89.1
1993.......	510	524	392	-	346	77.1	76.5	88.8	-	90.5
1994 [1].....	522	547	400	-	343	76.4	74.6	86.5	-	88.9
1995.......	538	566	411	-	350	75.5	73.3	86.4	-	87.1
1996.......	557	580	412	-	356	75.0	73.8	87.9	-	88.8
1997 [1].....	579	595	432	-	371	74.4	74.6	86.8	-	85.7
1998 [1].....	598	615	468	-	390	76.3	76.1	85.5	-	86.4
1999 [1].....	618	638	488	-	406	76.5	75.7	83.8	-	85.7
2000 [1].....	641	662	510	$685	417	76.9	75.8	84.1	79.9	87.8
2001.......	670	689	529	732	440	76.4	75.8	85.8	76.9	88.2
2002.......	679	702	524	756	451	77.9	77.9	90.3	74.9	88.0
2003 [1].....	695	715	555	772	464	79.4	79.3	88.5	77.5	88.4
2004.......	713	732	569	802	480	80.4	79.8	88.8	76.4	87.3
2005......	722	743	559	825	489	81.0	80.2	89.3	80.6	87.7
2006.......	743	761	591	882	505	80.8	80.0	87.8	79.3	87.1
2007.......	766	788	600	936	520	80.2	79.4	88.8	78.1	91.0
2008 [1].....	798	825	620	966	559	79.9	79.3	89.4	78.0	89.6

[1] The comparability of historical labor force data has been affected at various times by methodological and conceptual changes in the Current Population Survey (CPS). For an explanation, see the Historical Comparability documentation provided at http://www.bls.gov/cps/eetech_methods.pdf.

NOTE: Beginning in 2003, estimates for the above race groups (white, black or African American, and Asian) include persons who selected this race group only; persons who selected more than one race group are not included. Prior to 2003, persons who reported more than one race were included in the group they identified as the main race. Data for 2000-02 are for the category Asians and Pacific Islanders. Starting in 2003, Asians constitute a separate category. For more information, see the Historical Comparability documentation. Data for Asians were not tabulated prior to 2000.

SOURCE: Current Population Survey, U.S. Department of Labor, U.S. Bureau of Labor Statistics.

Table 17. **Median usual weekly earnings of full-time wage and salary workers 25 years and over by educational attainment and sex, 2008 annual averages**

Educational attainment and sex	Total employed (in thousands)	Median weekly earnings
Total, both sexes		
Total......	96,027	$761
Less than a high school diploma	8,120	453
High school graduate or more [1].........	87,907	800
High school graduates, no college [1]......	27,392	618
Some college or associate degree......	26,526	722
Some college, no degree............	16,522	699
Associate degree............	10,004	757
Occupational program............	4,541	750
Academic program............	5,463	762
College graduates, total............	33,990	1,115
Bachelor's degree............	22,033	1,012
Master's degree............	8,881	1,233
Professional degree............	1,620	1,531
Doctoral degree............	1,455	1,561
Women		
Total.........	42,584	670
Less than a high school diploma.........	2,566	378
High school graduate or more [1].........	40,018	697
High school graduates, no college [1]......	11,451	520
Some college or associate degree......	12,756	628
Some college, no degree............	7,713	611
Associate degree............	5,043	661
Occupational program............	2,121	639
Academic program............	2,922	676
College graduates, total............	15,812	955
Bachelor's degree............	10,202	878
Master's degree............	4,476	1,074
Professional degree............	629	1,258
Doctoral degree............	504	1,352

Table 17. **Median usual weekly earnings of full-time wage and salary workers 25 years and over by educational attainment and sex, 2008 annual averages—Continued**

Educational attainment and sex	Total employed (in thousands)	Median weekly earnings
Men		
Total..	53,444	$857
Less than a high school diploma............	5,554	497
High school graduate or more [1]............	47,889	913
High school graduates, no college [1]......	15,941	709
Some college or associate degree.........	13,770	830
Some college, no degree....................	8,809	803
Associate degree...........................	4,961	883
Occupational program.....................	2,420	871
Academic program........................	2,541	896
College graduates, total....................	18,178	1,285
Bachelor's degree.........................	11,831	1,172
Master's degree...........................	4,405	1,442
Professional degree.......................	991	1,758
Doctoral degree...........................	951	1,736

[1] Includes persons with a high school diploma or equivalent.

SOURCE: Current Population Survey, U.S. Department of Labor, U.S. Bureau of Labor Statistics.

Table 18. **Median usual weekly earnings of full-time wage and salary workers by detailed occupation and sex, 2008 annual averages**

(Numbers in thousands)

Occupation	Total, both sexes		Women		Men		Women's earnings as percent of men's
	Total employed	Median weekly earnings	Total employed	Median weekly earnings	Total employed	Median weekly earnings	
Total, 16 years and older..	106,648	$722	47,209	$638	59,439	$798	79.9
Management, professional, and related occupations......	40,154	1,025	20,535	892	19,619	1,238	72.1
Management, business, and financial operations occupations...	16,310	1,128	7,463	941	8,847	1,343	70.1
Management occupations..	11,223	1,204	4,535	979	6,687	1,384	70.7
Chief executives..	1,044	1,903	251	1,603	793	1,999	80.2
General and operations managers......................	919	1,229	274	993	646	1,315	75.5
Legislators..	16	(^{1})	7	(^{1})	9	(^{1})	(^{2})
Advertising and promotions managers................	69	1,097	52	1,000	17	(^{1})	(^{2})
Marketing and sales managers.........................	867	1,345	357	1,024	510	1,601	64.0
Public relations managers................................	57	1,232	31	(^{1})	26	(^{1})	(^{2})
Administrative services managers.....................	92	1,003	26	(^{1})	66	1,012	(^{2})
Computer and information systems managers......	431	1,576	120	1,260	311	1,641	76.8
Financial managers...	1,063	1,134	583	945	480	1,457	64.9
Human resources managers.............................	288	1,233	194	1,137	93	1,433	79.3
Industrial production managers.........................	222	1,253	30	(^{1})	192	1,285	(^{2})
Purchasing managers......................................	183	1,139	72	995	111	1,251	79.5
Transportation, storage, and distribution managers......................................	218	877	38	(^{1})	179	885	(^{2})
Farm, ranch, and other agricultural managers......	76	775	13	(^{1})	63	802	(^{2})
Construction managers....................................	586	1,189	49	(^{1})	536	1,219	(^{2})
Education administrators..................................	725	1,170	447	1,000	278	1,398	71.5
Engineering managers.....................................	99	1,752	5	(^{1})	95	1,758	(^{2})
Food service managers....................................	619	676	296	628	323	739	85.0
Funeral directors..	25	(^{1})	6	(^{1})	18	(^{1})	(^{2})
Gaming managers...	14	(^{1})	4	(^{1})	11	(^{1})	(^{2})
Lodging managers..	119	788	56	720	63	877	82.1
Medical and health services managers...............	500	1,170	351	1,066	150	1,504	70.9
Natural sciences managers...............................	15	(^{1})	2	(^{1})	12	(^{1})	(^{2})
Postmasters and mail superintendents...............	36	(^{1})	19	(^{1})	17	(^{1})	(^{2})
Property, real estate, and community association managers....................	303	847	177	758	128	1,054	71.9
Social and community service managers............	277	965	191	871	86	1,254	69.5
Managers, all other...	2,361	1,225	885	1,010	1,477	1,359	74.3
Business and financial operations occupations.......	5,087	974	2,928	885	2,159	1,167	75.8
Agents and business managers of artists, performers, and athletes...................	28	(^{1})	11	(^{1})	17	(^{1})	(^{2})
Purchasing agents and buyers, farm products......	5	(^{1})	3	(^{1})	2	(^{1})	(^{2})
Wholesale and retail buyers, except farm products......................................	152	816	70	801	82	826	97.0
Purchasing agents, except wholesale, retail, and farm products..	253	890	146	859	107	923	93.1
Claims adjusters, appraisers, examiners, and investigators...	286	810	188	766	99	891	86.0
Compliance officers, except agriculture, construction, health and safety, and transportation...	164	1,126	86	950	78	1,245	76.3
Cost estimators..	82	1,055	9	(^{1})	73	1,082	(^{2})
Human resources, training, and labor relations specialists..	717	918	504	850	213	1,158	73.4
Logisticians...	39	(^{1})	19	(^{1})	21	(^{1})	(^{2})
Management analysts......................................	454	1,255	209	1,139	245	1,391	81.9
Meeting and convention planners......................	47	(^{1})	37	(^{1})	10	(^{1})	(^{2})

See footnotes at end of table.

(Numbers in thousands)

Occupation	Total, both sexes		Women		Men		Women's earnings as percent of men's
	Total employed	Median weekly earnings	Total employed	Median weekly earnings	Total employed	Median weekly earnings	
Other business operations specialists.................	214	$931	145	$850	69	$1,157	73.5
Accountants and auditors....................	1,494	981	904	908	591	1,178	77.1
Appraisers and assessors of real estate.............	61	1,089	22	([1])	39	([1])	([2])
Budget analysts....................	62	1,197	37	([1])	26	([1])	([2])
Credit analysts....................	20	([1])	11	([1])	9	([1])	([2])
Financial analysts....................	84	1,378	39	([1])	45	([1])	([2])
Personal financial advisors....................	313	1,194	117	935	197	1,370	68.2
Insurance underwriters....................	77	957	62	917	15	([1])	([2])
Financial examiners....................	6	([1])	3	([1])	4	([1])	([2])
Loan counselors and officers....................	355	916	201	812	154	1,118	72.6
Tax examiners, collectors, and revenue agents....	53	850	35	([1])	18	([1])	([2])
Tax preparers....................	54	911	36	([1])	18	([1])	([2])
Financial specialists, all other....................	66	964	35	([1])	30	([1])	([2])
Professional and related occupations....................	23,845	980	13,072	867	10,773	1,169	74.2
Computer and mathematical occupations............	3,344	1,242	828	1,088	2,516	1,320	82.4
Computer scientists and systems analysts..........	752	1,184	213	1,082	538	1,240	87.3
Computer programmers....................	470	1,218	105	1,003	365	1,261	79.5
Computer software engineers....................	955	1,529	196	1,351	759	1,555	86.9
Computer support specialists....................	379	893	105	878	274	903	97.2
Database administrators....................	93	1,274	25	([1])	68	1,289	([2])
Network and computer systems administrators.....	212	1,189	46	([1])	166	1,209	([2])
Network systems and data communications analysts....................	353	1,130	82	961	271	1,184	81.2
Actuaries....................	24	([1])	6	([1])	18	([1])	([2])
Mathematicians....................	2	([1])	-	-	2	([1])	([2])
Operations research analysts....................	69	1,259	36	([1])	34	([1])	([2])
Statisticians....................	33	([1])	14	([1])	19	([1])	([2])
Miscellaneous mathematical science occupations....................	2	([1])	-	-	1	([1])	([2])
Architecture and engineering occupations............	2,652	1,244	334	1,001	2,319	1,286	77.8
Architects, except naval....................	150	1,128	35	([1])	115	1,273	([2])
Surveyors, cartographers, and photogrammetrists....................	34	([1])	3	([1])	32	([1])	([2])
Aerospace engineers....................	131	1,554	12	([1])	120	1,622	([2])
Agricultural engineers....................	4	([1])	-	-	4	([1])	([2])
Biomedical engineers....................	10	([1])	3	([1])	8	([1])	([2])
Chemical engineers....................	64	1,546	8	([1])	56	1,562	([2])
Civil engineers....................	303	1,332	36	([1])	268	1,349	([2])
Computer hardware engineers....................	62	1,258	14	([1])	48	([1])	([2])
Electrical and electronics engineers....................	334	1,443	26	([1])	307	1,475	([2])
Environmental engineers....................	29	([1])	8	([1])	21	([1])	([2])
Industrial engineers, including health and safety...	163	1,311	23	([1])	140	1,364	([2])
Marine engineers and naval architects....................	15	([1])	-	-	15	([1])	([2])
Materials engineers....................	41	([1])	6	([1])	35	([1])	([2])
Mechanical engineers....................	300	1,433	23	([1])	276	1,445	([2])
Mining and geological engineers, including mining safety engineers....................	12	([1])	1	([1])	10	([1])	([2])
Nuclear engineers....................	9	([1])	-	-	9	([1])	([2])
Petroleum engineers....................	18	([1])	1	([1])	17	([1])	([2])
Engineers, all other....................	347	1,418	39	([1])	308	1,425	([2])
Drafters....................	150	881	31	([1])	119	924	([2])
Engineering technicians, except drafters............	392	905	59	781	332	933	83.7
Surveying and mapping technicians....................	87	794	6	([1])	80	801	([2])

See footnotes at end of table.

Table 18. **Median usual weekly earnings of full-time wage and salary workers by detailed occupation and sex, 2008 annual averages—Continued**

(Numbers in thousands)

Occupation	Total, both sexes		Women		Men		Women's earnings as percent of men's
	Total employed	Median weekly earnings	Total employed	Median weekly earnings	Total employed	Median weekly earnings	
Life, physical, and social science occupations.........	1,080	$1,035	477	$931	603	$1,156	80.5
Agricultural and food scientists..........................	34	(1)	11	(1)	23	(1)	(2)
Biological scientists..	91	1,023	46	(1)	45	(1)	(2)
Conservation scientists and foresters................	21	(1)	2	(1)	18	(1)	(2)
Medical scientists..	120	989	60	948	60	1,133	83.7
Astronomers and physicists..............................	20	(1)	3	(1)	16	(1)	(2)
Atmospheric and space scientists.....................	8	(1)	2	(1)	6	(1)	(2)
Chemists and materials scientists.....................	103	1,118	38	(1)	65	1,430	(2)
Environmental scientists and geoscientists..........	70	1,253	22	(1)	48	(1)	(2)
Physical scientists, all other.............................	122	1,363	50	1,061	72	1,535	69.1
Economists..	17	(1)	4	(1)	13	(1)	(2)
Market and survey researchers.........................	109	1,071	60	990	49	(1)	(2)
Psychologists..	84	1,220	57	1,004	27	(1)	(2)
Sociologists..	1	(1)	1	(1)	-	-	(2)
Urban and regional planners.............................	31	(1)	17	(1)	13	(1)	(2)
Miscellaneous social scientists and related workers...	36	(1)	13	(1)	23	(1)	(2)
Agricultural and food science technicians...........	23	(1)	9	(1)	14	(1)	(2)
Biological technicians......................................	20	(1)	8	(1)	13	(1)	(2)
Chemical technicians.......................................	56	872	20	(1)	36	(1)	(2)
Geological and petroleum technicians...............	9	(1)	3	(1)	6	(1)	(2)
Nuclear technicians...	2	(1)	1	(1)	1	(1)	(2)
Other life, physical, and social science technicians..	103	752	50	752	54	751	100.1
Community and social services occupations..........	1,908	788	1,117	753	791	860	87.6
Counselors...	522	787	355	787	167	787	100.0
Social workers..	639	784	503	779	135	812	95.9
Miscellaneous community and social service specialists...	261	736	159	680	102	874	77.8
Clergy..	388	882	43	(1)	346	899	(2)
Directors, religious activities and education.........	38	(1)	21	(1)	18	(1)	(2)
Religious workers, all other..............................	60	669	36	(1)	24	(1)	(2)
Legal occupations...	1,199	1,174	693	962	506	1,696	56.7
Lawyers...	645	1,751	247	1,509	398	1,875	80.5
Judges, magistrates, and other judicial workers....	51	1,281	24	(1)	27	(1)	(2)
Paralegals and legal assistants.........................	304	796	267	790	37	(1)	(2)
Miscellaneous legal support workers..................	198	738	155	702	43	(1)	(2)
Education, training, and library occupations...........	6,677	866	4,883	818	1,794	1,020	80.2
Postsecondary teachers...................................	862	1,149	379	1,056	483	1,245	84.8
Preschool and kindergarten teachers.................	506	591	493	589	14	(1)	(2)
Elementary and middle school teachers.............	2,627	890	2,127	871	500	994	87.6
Secondary school teachers...............................	1,086	949	596	920	490	995	92.5
Special education teachers...............................	343	944	291	949	52	914	103.8
Other teachers and instructors..........................	351	858	209	812	142	953	85.2
Archivists, curators, and museum technicians......	25	(1)	13	(1)	11	(1)	(2)
Librarians...	136	878	111	811	25	(1)	(2)
Library technicians..	17	(1)	14	(1)	3	(1)	(2)
Teacher assistants..	651	421	595	413	56	517	79.9
Other education, training, and library workers......	74	1,071	55	886	19	(1)	(2)
Arts, design, entertainment, sports, and media occupations...	1,570	882	689	777	882	951	81.7
Artists and related workers...............................	74	985	23	(1)	51	1,103	(2)
Designers...	540	811	268	744	271	899	82.8

See footnotes at end of table.

(Numbers in thousands)

Occupation	Total, both sexes		Women		Men		Women's earnings as percent of men's
	Total employed	Median weekly earnings	Total employed	Median weekly earnings	Total employed	Median weekly earnings	
Actors...	2	(¹)	1	(¹)	1	(¹)	(²)
Producers and directors............................	108	$938	42	(¹)	65	$983	(²)
Athletes, coaches, umpires, and related workers...	117	825	25	(¹)	91	837	(²)
Dancers and choreographers.......................	13	(¹)	11	(¹)	1	(¹)	(²)
Musicians, singers, and related workers..........	32	(¹)	5	(¹)	27	(¹)	(²)
Entertainers and performers, sports and related workers, all other..................................	12	(¹)	3	(¹)	9	(¹)	(²)
Announcers...	22	(¹)	3	(¹)	19	(¹)	(²)
News analysts, reporters and correspondents......	68	947	25	(¹)	43	(¹)	(²)
Public relations specialists........................	107	1,000	70	$935	37	(¹)	(²)
Editors...	132	971	69	941	63	1,062	88.6
Technical writers....................................	48	(¹)	22	(¹)	26	(¹)	(²)
Writers and authors.................................	79	945	41	(¹)	38	(¹)	(²)
Miscellaneous media and communication workers	46	(¹)	33	(¹)	14	(¹)	(²)
Broadcast and sound engineering technicians and radio operators................................	75	972	13	(¹)	62	996	(²)
Photographers..	69	690	30	(¹)	39	(¹)	(²)
Television, video, and motion picture camera operators and editors..............................	26	(¹)	5	(¹)	21	(¹)	(²)
Media and communication equipment workers, all other..	1	(¹)	-	-	1	(¹)	(²)
Healthcare practitioner and technical occupations....	5,415	962	4,052	909	1,362	1,210	75.1
Chiropractors..	9	(¹)	2	(¹)	8	(¹)	(²)
Dentists...	34	(¹)	15	(¹)	19	(¹)	(²)
Dietitians and nutritionists........................	86	672	75	674	11	(¹)	(²)
Optometrists...	11	(¹)	5	(¹)	5	(¹)	(²)
Pharmacists..	196	1,883	94	1,647	102	1,914	86.1
Physicians and surgeons............................	594	1,731	189	1,230	405	1,911	64.4
Physician assistants.................................	86	1,251	51	1,077	34	(¹)	(²)
Podiatrists..	6	(¹)	1	(¹)	5	(¹)	(²)
Registered nurses...................................	2,114	1,022	1,904	1,011	210	1,168	86.6
Audiologists..	7	(¹)	5	(¹)	2	(¹)	(²)
Occupational therapists............................	55	1,019	54	1,016	1	(¹)	(²)
Physical therapists..................................	129	1,176	78	1,019	51	1,329	76.7
Radiation therapists................................	15	(¹)	10	(¹)	5	(¹)	(²)
Recreational therapists............................	16	(¹)	12	(¹)	5	(¹)	(²)
Respiratory therapists..............................	90	881	64	819	26	(¹)	(²)
Speech-language pathologists.....................	88	1,121	87	1,124	-	-	(²)
Therapists, all other................................	74	791	56	796	18	(¹)	(²)
Veterinarians..	26	(¹)	16	(¹)	10	(¹)	(²)
Health diagnosing and treating practitioners, all other..	3	(¹)	2	(¹)	-	-	(²)
Clinical laboratory technologists and technicians...	301	783	223	750	78	942	79.6
Dental hygienists...................................	75	976	73	988	2	(¹)	(²)
Diagnostic related technologists and technicians...	238	957	159	923	79	1,035	89.2
Emergency medical technicians and paramedics..	121	755	39	(1)	82	823	(²)
Health diagnosing and treating practitioner support technicians...............................	340	585	258	564	82	677	83.3
Licensed practical and licensed vocational nurses	439	692	408	679	31	(¹)	(²)
Medical records and health information technicians..	77	537	71	551	6	(¹)	(²)
Opticians, dispensing...............................	33	(¹)	23	(¹)	10	(¹)	(²)
Miscellaneous health technologists and technicians..	105	671	61	615	44	(¹)	(²)

See footnotes at end of table.

(Numbers in thousands)

Occupation	Total, both sexes		Women		Men		Women's earnings as percent of men's
	Total employed	Median weekly earnings	Total employed	Median weekly earnings	Total employed	Median weekly earnings	
Other healthcare practitioners and technical occupations...................	49	([1])	17	([1])	32	([1])	([2])
Service occupations.............................	14,814	$475	7,458	$418	7,355	$537	77.8
Healthcare support occupations............	2,222	465	1,951	459	271	512	89.6
Nursing, psychiatric, and home health aides........	1,370	429	1,201	424	169	485	87.4
Occupational therapist assistants and aides.........	7	([1])	6	([1])	1	([1])	([2])
Physical therapist assistants and aides..............	51	700	39	([1])	12	([1])	([2])
Massage therapists..........................	32	([1])	22	([1])	10	([1])	([2])
Dental assistants.............................	168	531	160	524	8	([1])	([2])
Medical assistants and other healthcare support occupations........................	595	505	524	502	71	529	94.9
Protective service occupations................	2,683	748	564	594	2,119	794	74.8
First-line supervisors/managers of correctional officers....................	43	([1])	16	([1])	27	([1])	([2])
First-line supervisors/managers of police and detectives....................	120	1,200	20	([1])	99	1,239	([2])
First-line supervisors/managers of fire fighting and prevention workers................	53	1,327	4	([1])	49	([1])	([2])
Supervisors, protective service workers, all other..	94	763	22	([1])	72	768	([2])
Fire fighters.................................	283	970	13	([1])	270	975	([2])
Fire inspectors..............................	24	([1])	-	-	24	([1])	([2])
Bailiffs, correctional officers, and jailers..............	387	695	112	605	275	725	83.4
Detectives and criminal investigators.................	139	1,053	28	([1])	112	1,112	([2])
Fish and game wardens.......................	4	([1])	-	-	4	([1])	([2])
Parking enforcement workers.................	5	([1])	4	([1])	1	([1])	([2])
Police and sheriff's patrol officers....................	674	893	101	731	573	929	78.7
Transit and railroad police.....................	3	([1])	-	-	3	([1])	([2])
Animal control workers.......................	9	([1])	3	([1])	6	([1])	([2])
Private detectives and investigators..................	76	780	28	([1])	47	([1])	([2])
Security guards and gaming surveillance officers..	695	516	173	478	523	540	88.5
Crossing guards.............................	20	([1])	17	([1])	3	([1])	([2])
Lifeguards and other protective service workers,,,	54	401	23	([1])	31	([1])	([2])
Food preparation and serving related occupations...	4,153	402	2,035	376	2,118	432	87.0
Chefs and head cooks.......................	295	548	40	([1])	255	551	([2])
First-line supervisors/managers of food preparation and serving workers...................	483	498	280	439	203	599	73.3
Cooks......................................	1,312	390	480	363	832	404	89.9
Food preparation workers....................	325	352	197	338	128	368	91.8
Bartenders.................................	204	502	108	457	96	596	76.7
Combined food preparation and serving workers, including fast food...................	141	349	99	341	42	([1])	([2])
Counter attendants, cafeteria, food concession, and coffee shop...................	84	307	54	299	30	([1])	([2])
Waiters and waitresses......................	852	391	560	367	292	436	84.2
Food servers, nonrestaurant.................	91	451	62	424	29	([1])	([2])
Dining room and cafeteria attendants and bartender helpers...................	159	390	69	386	90	394	98.0
Dishwashers................................	152	361	44	([1])	108	367	([2])
Hosts and hostesses, restaurant, lounge, and coffee shop...................	49	([1])	39	([1])	10	([1])	([2])
Food preparation and serving related workers, all other...................	6	([1])	4	([1])	2	([1])	([2])

See footnotes at end of table.

Table 18. **Median usual weekly earnings of full-time wage and salary workers by detailed occupation and sex, 2008 annual averages—Continued**

(Numbers in thousands)

Occupation	Total, both sexes		Women		Men		Women's earnings as percent of men's
	Total employed	Median weekly earnings	Total employed	Median weekly earnings	Total employed	Median weekly earnings	
Building and grounds cleaning and maintenance occupations....................	3,506	$431	1,274	$383	2,232	$488	78.5
First-line supervisors/managers of housekeeping and janitorial workers...............	200	623	74	448	127	748	59.9
First-line supervisors/managers of landscaping, lawn service, and groundskeeping workers........	86	687	4	([1])	82	712	([2])
Janitors and building cleaners..........................	1,510	460	414	397	1,096	493	80.5
Maids and housekeeping cleaners...................	847	378	742	371	105	436	85.1
Pest control workers............................	61	611	4	([1])	57	596	([2])
Grounds maintenance workers......................	802	420	37	([1])	766	422	([2])
Personal care and service occupations.................	2,250	475	1,634	441	615	591	74.6
First-line supervisors/managers of gaming workers..................	97	760	36	([1])	62	837	([2])
First-line supervisors/managers of personal service workers................	61	618	38	([1])	23	([1])	([2])
Animal trainers....................	12	([1])	6	([1])	6	([1])	([2])
Nonfarm animal caretakers.......................	62	457	45	([1])	18	([1])	([2])
Gaming services workers..........................	84	650	43	([1])	41	([1])	([2])
Motion picture projectionists....................	5	([1])	-	-	5	([1])	([2])
Ushers, lobby attendants, and ticket takers..........	7	([1])	3	([1])	4	([1])	([2])
Miscellaneous entertainment attendants and related workers.....................	70	415	34	([1])	36	([1])	([2])
Funeral service workers......................	6	([1])	1	([1])	5	([1])	([2])
Barbers..........................	38	([1])	7	([1])	31	([1])	([2])
Hairdressers, hairstylists, and cosmetologists......	306	496	269	489	37	([1])	([2])
Miscellaneous personal appearance workers.......	130	462	102	444	28	([1])	([2])
Baggage porters, bellhops, and concierges.........	55	581	11	([1])	44	([1])	([2])
Tour and travel guides.......................	20	([1])	11	([1])	9	([1])	([2])
Transportation attendants....................	102	717	68	637	34	([1])	([2])
Child care workers................................	435	396	410	393	25	([1])	([2])
Personal and home care aides..........................	485	414	394	404	91	475	85.1
Recreation and fitness workers......................	176	514	105	487	70	639	76.2
Residential advisors.............................	52	584	32	([1])	20	([1])	([2])
Personal care and service workers, all other........	46	([1])	18	([1])	28	([1])	([2])
Sales and office occupations............................	25,232	614	15,635	578	9,597	733	78.9
Sales and related occupations............................	10,113	656	4,518	516	5,594	796	64.8
First-line supervisors/managers of retail sales workers......................	2,432	669	1,050	556	1,382	781	71.2
First-line supervisors/managers of non-retail sales workers......................	788	882	233	765	555	947	80.8
Cashiers..........................	1,376	360	1,018	349	359	399	87.5
Counter and rental clerks......................	93	586	35	([1])	58	671	([2])
Parts salespersons...........................	111	519	12	([1])	99	555	([2])
Retail salespersons..........................	1,996	521	848	440	1,148	623	70.6
Advertising sales agents.......................	181	838	99	804	82	879	91.5
Insurance sales agents........................	379	767	198	652	182	994	65.6
Securities, commodities, and financial services sales agents........................	290	1,127	84	760	206	1,272	59.7
Travel agents............................	64	685	45	([1])	19	([1])	([2])
Sales representatives, services, all other............	431	926	148	841	283	957	87.9
Sales representatives, wholesale and manufacturing......................	1,143	986	299	846	844	1,064	79.5

See footnotes at end of table.

Table 18. **Median usual weekly earnings of full-time wage and salary workers by detailed occupation and sex, 2008 annual averages—Continued**

(Numbers in thousands)

Occupation	Total, both sexes		Women		Men		Women's earnings as percent of men's
	Total employed	Median weekly earnings	Total employed	Median weekly earnings	Total employed	Median weekly earnings	
Models, demonstrators, and product promoters....	25	(¹)	18	(¹)	8	(¹)	(²)
Real estate brokers and sales agents...............	462	$794	251	$682	211	$952	71.6
Sales engineers...	41	(¹)	2	(¹)	39	(¹)	(²)
Telemarketers...	95	457	61	473	34	(¹)	(²)
Door-to-door salesworkers, news and street vendors, and related workers.....................	55	507	26	(¹)	29	(¹)	(²)
Sales and related workers, all other...............	149	746	90	695	58	809	85.9
Office and administrative support occupations........	15,119	601	11,117	590	4,003	651	90.6
First-line supervisors/managers of office and administrative support workers.......................	1,500	731	1,029	688	470	848	81.1
Switchboard operators, including answering service...	40	(¹)	34	(¹)	6	(¹)	(²)
Telephone operators......................................	37	(¹)	27	(¹)	10	(¹)	(²)
Communications equipment operators, all other...	7	(¹)	4	(¹)	3	(¹)	(²)
Bill and account collectors.............................	206	605	139	597	67	618	96.6
Billing and posting clerks and machine operators..	428	584	386	575	42	(1)	(²)
Bookkeeping, accounting, and auditing clerks......	950	606	865	603	85	645	93.5
Gaming cage workers...................................	15	(¹)	13	(¹)	2	(¹)	(²)
Payroll and timekeeping clerks......................	127	690	110	700	17	(¹)	(²)
Procurement clerks......................................	23	(¹)	15	(¹)	8	(¹)	(²)
Tellers..	338	469	284	468	54	471	99.4
Brokerage clerks..	3	(¹)	3	(¹)	-	-	(²)
Correspondence clerks..................................	7	(¹)	4	(¹)	3	(¹)	(²)
Court, municipal, and license clerks................	92	673	70	643	22	(¹)	(²)
Credit authorizers, checkers, and clerks...........	58	556	39	(¹)	19	(¹)	(²)
Customer service representatives....................	1,511	577	1,015	568	496	607	93.6
Eligibility interviewers, government programs.......	60	665	50	668	9	(¹)	(²)
File clerks...	259	549	217	536	42	(¹)	(²)
Hotel, motel, and resort desk clerks................	81	410	58	406	24	(¹)	(²)
Interviewers, except eligibility and loan..............	110	581	88	573	22	(¹)	(²)
Library assistants, clerical..............................	41	(¹)	35	(¹)	6	(¹)	(²)
Loan interviewers and clerks...........................	114	681	97	643	17	(¹)	(²)
New accounts clerks......................................	24	(¹)	20	(¹)	3	(¹)	(²)
Order clerks...	98	548	54	541	45	(¹)	(²)
Human resources assistants, except payroll and timekeeping...	48	(¹)	40	(¹)	9	(¹)	(²)
Receptionists and information clerks.................	960	503	896	502	64	537	93.5
Reservation and transportation ticket agents and travel clerks..	120	572	70	538	50	752	71.5
Information and record clerks, all other..............	94	639	87	624	7	(¹)	(²)
Cargo and freight agents................................	17	(¹)	5	(¹)	12	(¹)	(²)
Couriers and messengers...............................	178	724	24	(¹)	154	755	(²)
Dispatchers...	243	653	134	578	109	722	80.1
Meter readers, utilities..................................	42	(¹)	6	(¹)	36	(¹)	(²)
Postal service clerks.....................................	157	877	80	853	77	905	94.3
Postal service mail carriers............................	338	908	101	803	237	939	85.5
Postal service mail sorters, processors, and processing machine operators.......................	84	830	35	(¹)	49	(¹)	(²)
Production, planning, and expediting clerks.........	249	750	147	690	102	862	80.0
Shipping, receiving, and traffic clerks................	478	543	140	516	338	559	92.3
Stock clerks and order fillers..........................	1,059	468	371	466	688	470	99.1
Weighers, measurers, checkers, and samplers, recordkeeping...	59	604	26	(¹)	34	(¹)	(²)
Secretaries and administrative assistants...........	2,575	616	2,485	614	90	736	83.4

See footnotes at end of table.

Table 18. **Median usual weekly earnings of full-time wage and salary workers by detailed occupation and sex, 2008 annual averages—Continued**

(Numbers in thousands)

Occupation	Total, both sexes		Women		Men		Women's earnings as percent of men's
	Total employed	Median weekly earnings	Total employed	Median weekly earnings	Total employed	Median weekly earnings	
Computer operators................................	112	$673	58	$632	55	$749	84.4
Data entry keyers..................................	339	586	261	565	77	652	86.7
Word processors and typists...................	112	571	102	560	10	([1])	([2])
Desktop publishers...............................	3	([1])	3	([1])	1	([1])	([2])
Insurance claims and policy processing clerks......	264	593	219	588	44	([1])	([2])
Mail clerks and mail machine operators, except postal service........................	98	494	50	446	48	([1])	([2])
Office clerks, general............................	840	585	727	582	113	602	96.7
Office machine operators, except computer.........	30	([1])	15	([1])	15	([1])	([2])
Proofreaders and copy markers................	11	([1])	8	([1])	4	([1])	([2])
Statistical assistants............................	18	([1])	14	([1])	4	([1])	([2])
Office and administrative support workers, all other....................................	464	657	357	636	107	729	87.2
Natural resources, construction, and maintenance occupations.....................	11,609	702	450	607	11,159	705	86.1
Farming, fishing, and forestry occupations............	756	420	144	392	612	427	91.8
First-line supervisors/managers of farming, fishing, and forestry workers................	35	([1])	4	([1])	31	([1])	([2])
Agricultural inspectors..........................	28	([1])	14	([1])	14	([1])	([2])
Animal breeders..................................	4	([1])	3	([1])	1	([1])	([2])
Graders and sorters, agricultural products..........	63	463	39	([1])	24	([1])	([2])
Miscellaneous agricultural workers................	564	394	83	346	481	402	86.1
Fishers and related fishing workers.............	9	([1])	-	-	9	([1])	([2])
Hunters and trappers...........................	1	([1])	-	-	1	([1])	([2])
Forest and conservation workers..............	5	([1])	1	([1])	4	([1])	([2])
Logging workers..................................	47	([1])	-	-	47	([1])	([2])
Construction and extraction occupations..............	6,432	688	139	747	6,293	688	108.6
First-line supervisors/managers of construction trades and extraction workers........	631	947	15	([1])	615	945	([2])
Boilermakers......................................	23	([1])	-	-	23	([1])	([2])
Brickmasons, blockmasons, and stonemasons.....	161	622	1	([1])	160	624	([2])
Carpenters..	986	656	11	([1])	975	655	([2])
Carpet, floor, and tile installers and finishers........	118	621	2	([1])	116	613	([2])
Cement masons, concrete finishers, and terrazzo workers...............................	77	574	-	-	77	574	([2])
Construction laborers...........................	1,210	564	31	([1])	1,180	558	([2])
Paving, surfacing, and tamping equipment operators.................................	23	([1])	3	([1])	20	([1])	([2])
Pile-driver operators............................	2	([1])	-	-	2	([1])	([2])
Operating engineers and other construction equipment operators........................	360	749	6	([1])	354	744	([2])
Drywall installers, ceiling tile installers, and tapers.	158	559	3	([1])	154	556	([2])
Electricians.......................................	728	807	6	([1])	722	809	([2])
Glaziers...	41	([1])	-	-	41	([1])	([2])
Insulation workers...............................	35	([1])	3	([1])	31	([1])	([2])
Painters, construction and maintenance............	386	554	20	([1])	366	556	([2])
Paperhangers....................................	4	([1])	-	-	4	([1])	([2])
Pipelayers, plumbers, pipefitters, and steamfitters.	492	784	8	([1])	484	785	([2])
Plasterers and stucco masons.................	42	([1])	-	-	42	([1])	([2])
Reinforcing iron and rebar workers...........	15	([1])	-	-	15	([1])	([2])
Roofers..	153	558	1	([1])	152	560	([2])
Sheet metal workers............................	112	732	7	([1])	105	733	([2])
Structural iron and steel workers.............	71	871	-	-	71	871	([2])
Helpers, construction trades...................	94	504	5	([1])	89	500	([2])

See footnotes at end of table.

Table 18. Median usual weekly earnings of full-time wage and salary workers by detailed occupation and sex, 2008 annual averages—Continued

(Numbers in thousands)

Occupation	Total, both sexes		Women		Men		Women's earnings as percent of men's
	Total employed	Median weekly earnings	Total employed	Median weekly earnings	Total employed	Median weekly earnings	
Construction and building inspectors.................	84	$854	7	(¹)	77	$849	(²)
Elevator installers and repairers......................	39	(¹)	3	(¹)	36	(¹)	(²)
Fence erectors.......................................	26	(¹)	-	-	26	(¹)	(²)
Hazardous materials removal workers...............	19	(¹)	2	(¹)	17	(¹)	(²)
Highway maintenance workers.......................	97	659	1	(¹)	96	656	(²)
Rail-track laying and maintenance equipment operators..	16	(¹)	-	-	16	(¹)	(²)
Septic tank servicers and sewer pipe cleaners......	9	(¹)	-	-	9	(¹)	(²)
Miscellaneous construction and related workers...	24	(¹)	-	-	24	(¹)	(²)
Derrick, rotary drill, and service unit operators, oil, gas, and mining............................	36	(¹)	1	(¹)	36	(¹)	(²)
Earth drillers, except oil and gas.....................	37	(¹)	-	-	37	(¹)	(²)
Explosives workers, ordnance handling experts, and blasters.................................	10	(¹)	-	-	9	(¹)	(²)
Mining machine operators............................	49	(¹)	1	(¹)	48	(¹)	(²)
Roof bolters, mining..................................	4	(¹)	-	-	4	(¹)	(²)
Roustabouts, oil and gas.............................	8	(¹)	-	-	8	(¹)	(²)
Helpers—extraction workers.........................	6	(¹)	-	-	6	(¹)	(²)
Other extraction workers............................	47	(¹)	1	(¹)	47	(¹)	(²)
Installation, maintenance, and repair occupations....	4,420	774	167	$779	4,253	774	100.6
First-line supervisors/managers of mechanics, installers, and repairers......................	297	937	24	(¹)	273	940	(²)
Computer, automated teller, and office machine repairers..................................	271	823	31	(¹)	240	805	(²)
Radio and telecommunications equipment installers and repairers......................	199	866	27	(¹)	172	881	(²)
Avionics technicians.................................	15	(¹)	2	(¹)	13	(¹)	(²)
Electric motor, power tool, and related repairers...	19	(¹)	2	(¹)	17	(¹)	(²)
Electrical and electronics installers and repairers, transportation equipment.................	5	(¹)	-	-	5	(¹)	(²)
Electrical and electronics repairers, industrial and utility..................................	18	(¹)	-	-	17	(¹)	(²)
Electronic equipment installers and repairers, motor vehicles..............................	26	(¹)	1	(¹)	25	(¹)	(²)
Electronic home entertainment equipment installers and repairers......................	52	787	1	(¹)	51	796	(²)
Security and fire alarm systems installers...........	50	745	-	-	50	745	(²)
Aircraft mechanics and service technicians.........	144	919	3	(¹)	141	928	(²)
Automotive body and related repairers..............	116	713	1	(¹)	115	715	(²)
Automotive glass installers and repairers...........	26	(¹)	-	-	26	(¹)	(²)
Automotive service technicians and mechanics....	650	677	9	(¹)	641	678	(²)
Bus and truck mechanics and diesel engine specialists.................................	328	763	2	(¹)	326	763	(²)
Heavy vehicle and mobile equipment service technicians and mechanics....................	202	846	2	(¹)	200	847	(²)
Small engine mechanics..............................	44	(¹)	1	(¹)	43	(¹)	(²)
Miscellaneous vehicle and mobile equipment mechanics, installers, and repairers.................	69	489	-	-	69	489	(²)
Control and valve installers and repairers...........	22	(¹)	-	-	22	(¹)	(²)
Heating, air conditioning, and refrigeration mechanics and installers.....................	311	804	5	(¹)	306	805	(²)
Home appliance repairers............................	31	(¹)	-	-	31	(¹)	(²)
Industrial and refractory machinery mechanics.....	419	801	12	(¹)	407	806	(²)
Maintenance and repair workers, general..........	420	720	16	(¹)	404	719	(²)

See footnotes at end of table.

Table 18. Median usual weekly earnings of full-time wage and salary workers by detailed occupation and sex, 2008 annual averages—Continued

(Numbers in thousands)

Occupation	Total, both sexes		Women		Men		Women's earnings as percent of men's
	Total employed	Median weekly earnings	Total employed	Median weekly earnings	Total employed	Median weekly earnings	
Maintenance workers, machinery	40	(¹)	-	-	40	(¹)	(²)
Millwrights	65	$956	1	(¹)	64	$960	(²)
Electrical power-line installers and repairers	97	1,093	1	(¹)	96	1,090	(²)
Telecommunications line installers and repairers	187	848	7	(¹)	181	836	(²)
Precision instrument and equipment repairers	46	(¹)	6	(¹)	40	(¹)	(²)
Coin, vending, and amusement machine servicers and repairers	31	(¹)	4	(¹)	27	(¹)	(²)
Commercial divers	1	(¹)	-	-	1	(¹)	(²)
Locksmiths and safe repairers	21	(¹)	1	(¹)	20	(¹)	(²)
Manufactured building and mobile home installers	7	(¹)	1	(¹)	6	(¹)	(²)
Riggers	7	(¹)	-	-	7	(¹)	(²)
Signal and track switch repairers	5	(¹)	-	-	5	(¹)	(²)
Helpers—installation, maintenance, and repair workers	16	(¹)	-	-	16	(¹)	(²)
Other installation, maintenance, and repair workers	166	639	9	(¹)	156	638	(²)
Production, transportation, and material moving occupations	14,840	594	3,131	$462	11,709	637	72.5
Production occupations	8,008	595	2,245	464	5,763	659	70.4
First-line supervisors/managers of production and operating workers	810	857	140	634	671	899	70.5
Aircraft structure, surfaces, rigging, and systems assemblers	23	(¹)	6	(¹)	16	(¹)	(²)
Electrical, electronics, and electromechanical assemblers	185	506	107	453	78	600	75.5
Engine and other machine assemblers	14	(¹)	3	(¹)	11	(¹)	(²)
Structural metal fabricators and fitters	29	(¹)	-	-	29	(¹)	(²)
Miscellaneous assemblers and fabricators	959	531	337	466	622	581	80.2
Bakers	143	426	68	393	75	478	82.2
Butchers and other meat, poultry, and fish processing workers	303	490	81	430	223	512	84.0
Food and tobacco roasting, baking, and drying machine operators and tenders	10	(¹)	5	(¹)	5	(¹)	(²)
Food batchmakers	66	477	34	(¹)	32	(¹)	(²)
Food cooking machine operators and tenders	5	(¹)	2	(¹)	3	(¹)	(²)
Computer control programmers and operators	65	810	6	(¹)	59	820	(²)
Extruding and drawing machine setters, operators, and tenders, metal and plastic	9	(¹)	-	-	9	(¹)	(²)
Forging machine setters, operators, and tenders, metal and plastic	10	(¹)	-	-	10	(¹)	(²)
Rolling machine setters, operators, and tenders, metal and plastic	12	(¹)	1	(¹)	11	(¹)	(²)
Cutting, punching, and press machine setters, operators, and tenders, metal and plastic	104	525	22	(¹)	82	548	(²)
Drilling and boring machine tool setters, operators, and tenders, metal and plastic	2	(¹)	1	(¹)	2	(¹)	(²)
Grinding, lapping, polishing, and buffing machine tool setters, operators, and tenders, metal and plastic	52	690	8	(¹)	44	(¹)	(²)
Lathe and turning machine tool setters, operators, and tenders, metal and plastic	23	(¹)	3	(¹)	20	(¹)	(²)
Milling and planing machine setters, operators, and tenders, metal and plastic	6	(¹)	1	(¹)	5	(¹)	(²)
Machinists	376	708	25	(¹)	351	715	(²)

See footnotes at end of table.

(Numbers in thousands)

Occupation	Total, both sexes		Women		Men		Women's earnings as percent of men's
	Total employed	Median weekly earnings	Total employed	Median weekly earnings	Total employed	Median weekly earnings	
Metal furnace and kiln operators and tenders........	25	(¹)	1	(¹)	24	(¹)	(²)
Model makers and patternmakers, metal and plastic..................	9	(¹)	-	-	9	(¹)	(²)
Molders and molding machine setters, operators, and tenders, metal and plastic..........	52	$589	11	(¹)	40	(¹)	(²)
Multiple machine tool setters, operators, and tenders, metal and plastic.............................	3	(¹)	2	(¹)	1	(¹)	(²)
Tool and die makers........................	64	946	1	(¹)	64	$952	(²)
Welding, soldering, and brazing workers............	536	666	22	(¹)	514	673	(²)
Heat treating equipment setters, operators, and tenders, metal and plastic........................	10	(¹)	3	(¹)	7	(¹)	(²)
Lay-out workers, metal and plastic...................	8	(¹)	1	(¹)	7	(¹)	(²)
Plating and coating machine setters, operators, and tenders, metal and plastic...................	12	(¹)	1	(¹)	11	(¹)	(²)
Tool grinders, filers, and sharpeners.................	5	(¹)	-	-	5	(¹)	(²)
Metalworkers and plastic workers, all other..........	356	586	73	$515	283	605	85.1
Bookbinders and bindery workers....................	29	(¹)	12	(¹)	17	(¹)	(²)
Job printers..................................	36	(¹)	5	(¹)	30	(¹)	(²)
Prepress technicians and workers....................	37	(¹)	20	(¹)	17	(¹)	(²)
Printing machine operators....................	197	631	40	(¹)	157	669	(²)
Laundry and dry-cleaning workers....................	179	362	106	345	73	414	83.3
Pressers, textile, garment, and related materials...	47	(¹)	37	(¹)	9	(¹)	(²)
Sewing machine operators.........................	175	386	131	383	45	(¹)	(²)
Shoe and leather workers and repairers.............	3	(¹)	-	-	3	(¹)	(²)
Shoe machine operators and tenders................	3	(¹)	2	(¹)	-	-	(²)
Tailors, dressmakers, and sewers.....................	25	(¹)	20	(¹)	5	(¹)	(²)
Textile bleaching and dyeing machine operators and tenders.................	3	(¹)	-	-	3	(¹)	(²)
Textile cutting machine setters, operators, and tenders.................	4	(¹)	1	(¹)	3	(¹)	(²)
Textile knitting and weaving machine setters, operators, and tenders.................	3	(¹)	1	(¹)	2	(¹)	(²)
Textile winding, twisting, and drawing out machine setters, operators, and tenders............	11	(¹)	8	(¹)	3	(¹)	(²)
Extruding and forming machine setters, operators, and tenders, synthetic and glass fibers............	3	(¹)	1	(¹)	2	(¹)	(²)
Fabric and apparel patternmakers....................	2	(¹)	2	(¹)	-	-	(²)
Upholsterers..................................	30	(¹)	7	(¹)	23	(¹)	(²)
Textile, apparel, and furnishings workers, all other	20	(¹)	6	(¹)	14	(¹)	(²)
Cabinetmakers and bench carpenters................	61	641	4	(¹)	57	655	(²)
Furniture finishers..........................	9	(¹)	2	(¹)	7	(¹)	(²)
Sawing machine setters, operators, and tenders, wood.................	38	(¹)	2	(¹)	35	(¹)	(²)
Woodworking machine setters, operators, and tenders, except sawing...............	18	(¹)	6	(¹)	12	(¹)	(²)
Woodworkers, all other...................	17	(¹)	4	(¹)	13	(¹)	(²)
Power plant operators, distributors, and dispatchers..................	53	960	6	(¹)	47	(¹)	(²)
Stationary engineers and boiler operators..........	97	848	1	(¹)	96	849	(²)
Water and liquid waste treatment plant and system operators...................	73	705	4	(¹)	69	693	(²)
Miscellaneous plant and system operators..........	34	(¹)	1	(¹)	33	(¹)	(²)
Chemical processing machine setters, operators, and tenders.................	51	918	6	(¹)	45	(¹)	(²)

See footnotes at end of table.

Table 18. **Median usual weekly earnings of full-time wage and salary workers by detailed occupation and sex, 2008 annual averages—Continued**

(Numbers in thousands)

Occupation	Total, both sexes		Women		Men		Women's earnings as percent of men's
	Total employed	Median weekly earnings	Total employed	Median weekly earnings	Total employed	Median weekly earnings	
Crushing, grinding, polishing, mixing, and blending workers..................................	106	$596	18	(¹)	88	$576	(²)
Cutting workers...	72	502	18	(¹)	55	514	(²)
Extruding, forming, pressing, and compacting machine setters, operators, and tenders............	29	(¹)	8	(¹)	21	(¹)	(²)
Furnace, kiln, oven, drier, and kettle operators and tenders.....................	11	(¹)	3	(¹)	8	(¹)	(²)
Inspectors, testers, sorters, samplers, and weighers.......................................	711	660	301	$527	409	765	68.9
Jewelers and precious stone and metal workers...	28	(¹)	13	(¹)	16	(¹)	(²)
Medical, dental, and ophthalmic laboratory technicians...	73	582	39	(¹)	34	(¹)	(²)
Packaging and filling machine operators and tenders..	240	449	131	401	109	501	80.0
Painting workers..	163	565	19	(¹)	144	579	(²)
Photographic process workers and processing machine operators..............................	32	(¹)	16	(¹)	16	(¹)	(²)
Semiconductor processors..........................	5	(¹)	3	(¹)	2	(¹)	(²)
Cementing and gluing machine operators and tenders..	9	(¹)	3	(¹)	6	(¹)	(²)
Cleaning, washing, and metal pickling equipment operators and tenders.....................	2	(¹)	-	-	2	(¹)	(²)
Cooling and freezing equipment operators and tenders..	1	(¹)	-	-	1	(¹)	(²)
Etchers and engravers................................	3	(¹)	1	(¹)	2	(¹)	(²)
Molders, shapers, and casters, except metal and plastic..	33	(¹)	3	(¹)	30	(¹)	(²)
Paper goods machine setters, operators, and tenders..	41	(¹)	12	(¹)	29	(¹)	(²)
Tire builders...	12	(¹)	3	(¹)	9	(¹)	(²)
Helpers—production workers........................	31	(¹)	5	(¹)	26	(¹)	(²)
Production workers, all other........................	866	545	251	485	615	592	81.9
Transportation and material moving occupations......	6,832	593	886	455	5,946	615	74.0
Supervisors, transportation and material moving workers.................................	215	761	38	(¹)	177	796	(²)
Aircraft pilots and flight engineers.................	92	1,390	4	(¹)	88	1,399	(²)
Air traffic controllers and airfield operations specialists...	26	(¹)	7	(¹)	19	(¹)	(²)
Ambulance drivers and attendants, except emergency medical technicians....................	16	(¹)	4	(¹)	12	(¹)	(²)
Bus drivers..	372	561	171	507	201	605	83.8
Driver/salesworkers and truck drivers..............	2,729	702	116	542	2,613	709	76.4
Taxi drivers and chauffeurs.........................	208	503	30	(¹)	179	514	(²)
Motor vehicle operators, all other...................	33	(¹)	6	(¹)	27	(¹)	(²)
Locomotive engineers and operators...............	53	1,223	2	(¹)	51	1,207	(²)
Railroad brake, signal, and switch operators........	5	(¹)	-	-	5	(¹)	(²)
Railroad conductors and yardmasters..............	53	1,067	2	(¹)	51	1,080	(²)
Subway, streetcar, and other rail transportation workers...	22	(¹)	5	(¹)	16	(¹)	(²)
Sailors and marine oilers............................	13	(¹)	-	-	13	(¹)	(²)
Ship and boat captains and operators..............	36	(¹)	3	(¹)	33	(¹)	(²)
Ship engineers...	4	(¹)	-	-	4	(¹)	(²)
Bridge and lock tenders..............................	7	(¹)	2	(¹)	5	(¹)	(²)
Parking lot attendants...............................	50	436	3	(¹)	46	(¹)	(²)

See footnotes at end of table.

(Numbers in thousands)

Occupation	Total, both sexes		Women		Men		Women's earnings as percent of men's
	Total employed	Median weekly earnings	Total employed	Median weekly earnings	Total employed	Median weekly earnings	
Service station attendants..................................	64	$373	7	([1])	56	$378	([2])
Transportation inspectors................................	44	([1])	7	([1])	37	([1])	([2])
Other transportation workers............................	13	([1])	2	([1])	11	([1])	([2])
Conveyor operators and tenders........................	6	([1])	-	-	6	([1])	([2])
Crane and tower operators...............................	68	925	2	([1])	66	933	([2])
Dredge, excavating, and loading machine operators..	41	([1])	1	([1])	39	([1])	([2])
Hoist and winch operators...............................	4	([1])	-	-	4	([1])	([2])
Industrial truck and tractor operators................	551	534	40	([1])	511	533	([2])
Cleaners of vehicles and equipment..................	227	428	19	([1])	208	437	([2])
Laborers and freight, stock, and material movers, hand..	1,392	501	198	$417	1,194	508	82.1
Machine feeders and offbearers........................	29	([1])	13	([1])	16	([1])	([2])
Packers and packagers, hand...........................	315	388	186	368	129	410	89.8
Pumping station operators...............................	23	([1])	1	([1])	22	([1])	([2])
Refuse and recyclable material collectors...........	70	475	10	([1])	61	493	([2])
Shuttle car operators......................................	5	([1])	-	-	5	([1])	([2])
Tank car, truck, and ship loaders......................	4	([1])	-	-	4	([1])	([2])
Material moving workers, all other.....................	43	([1])	8	([1])	35	([1])	([2])

[1] Data not shown where the employment base is less than 50,000.

[2] Data not shown where the employment base for either the numerator or denominator is less than 50,000.

NOTE: Dash indicates no data or data that do not meet publication criteria.

SOURCE: Current Population Survey, U.S. Department of Labor, U.S. Bureau of Labor Statistics.

Table 19. Median usual weekly earnings of full-time wage and salary workers by industry and sex, 2008 annual averages

Industry	Total, both sexes		Women		Men		Women's earnings as percent of men's
	Total employed	Median weekly earnings	Total employed	Median weekly earnings	Total employed	Median weekly earnings	
Total, 16 years and over...........................	106,648	$722	47,209	$638	59,439	$798	79.9
Agriculture and related industries	944	462	171	436	773	469	93.0
Mining	764	1,007	88	814	676	1,042	78.1
Construction	7,489	715	679	672	6,810	719	93.5
Manufacturing	14,548	743	4,112	601	10,437	811	74.1
Durable goods	9,435	774	2,322	633	7,113	834	75.9
Nondurable goods	5,114	686	1,790	563	3,324	764	73.7
Wholesale and retail trade	14,204	603	5,637	510	8,566	683	74.7
Wholesale trade	3,364	741	942	674	2,422	769	87.6
Retail trade	10,840	565	4,695	486	6,144	642	75.7
Transportation and utilities	6,377	811	1,387	684	4,990	859	79.6
Transportation and warehousing	5,178	775	1,155	662	4,023	812	81.5
Utilities	1,199	1,005	232	820	967	1,066	76.9
Information	2,822	891	1,130	761	1,692	999	76.2
Financial activities	7,988	814	4,495	712	3,493	1,015	70.1
Finance and insurance	6,163	856	3,669	726	2,495	1,171	62.0
Real estate and rental and leasing	1,825	704	826	653	999	750	87.1
Professional and business services	10,733	839	4,437	724	6,296	954	75.9
Professional and technical services	6,647	1,065	2,867	859	3,780	1,268	67.7
Management, administrative, and waste services...	4,085	550	1,569	521	2,516	569	91.6
Education and health services	23,324	739	17,264	690	6,060	910	75.8
Educational services	10,108	828	6,963	775	3,145	939	82.5
Health care and social assistance	13,216	667	10,301	628	2,915	869	72.3
Leisure and hospitality	7,036	477	3,214	421	3,822	510	82.5
Arts, entertainment, and recreation	1,613	594	645	522	967	647	80.7
Accomodation and food services	5,423	436	2,569	400	2,855	483	82.8
Other services	4,058	610	1,798	516	2,260	698	73.9
Other services, except private households ..	3,660	629	1,444	555	2,215	700	79.3
Private households	398	419	353	406	45	(^{1})	(^{1})
Public administration..................................	6,362	887	2,798	756	3,563	993	76.1

[1] Data not shown where the employment base is less than 50,000.

SOURCE: Current Population Survey, U.S. Department of Labor, U.S. Bureau of Labor Statistics.

Table 20. **Employed persons by full- and part-time status and sex, 1970-2008 annual averages**

(Numbers in thousands)

Year	Total, both sexes				
	Total employed	Usually full time [1]	Usually part time [2]	Percent usually full time	Percent usually part time
1970................	78,678	66,753	11,925	84.8	15.2
1971................	79,367	66,973	12,393	84.4	15.6
1972 [3]................	82,153	69,214	12,939	84.3	15.7
1973 [3]................	85,064	71,803	13,262	84.4	15.6
1974................	86,794	73,093	13,701	84.2	15.8
1975................	85,846	71,586	14,260	83.4	16.6
1976................	88,752	73,964	14,788	83.3	16.7
1977................	92,017	76,625	15,391	83.3	16.7
1978 [3]................	96,048	80,193	15,855	83.5	16.5
1979................	98,824	82,654	16,171	83.6	16.4
1980................	99,303	82,562	16,740	83.1	16.9
1981................	100,397	83,243	17,154	82.9	17.1
1982................	99,526	81,421	18,106	81.8	18.2
1983................	100,834	82,322	18,511	81.6	18.4
1984................	105,005	86,544	18,462	82.4	17.6
1985................	107,150	88,534	18,615	82.6	17.4
1986 [3]................	109,597	90,529	19,069	82.6	17.4
1987................	112,440	92,957	19,483	82.7	17.3
1988................	114,968	95,214	19,754	82.8	17.2
1989................	117,342	97,369	19,973	83.0	17.0
1990 [3]................	118,793	98,666	20,128	83.1	16.9
1991................	117,718	97,190	20,528	82.6	17.4
1992................	118,492	97,664	20,828	82.4	17.6
1993................	120,259	99,114	21,145	82.4	17.6
1994 [3]................	123,060	99,772	23,288	81.1	18.9
1995................	124,900	101,679	23,220	81.4	18.6
1996................	126,708	103,537	23,170	81.7	18.3
1997 [3]................	129,558	106,334	23,224	82.1	17.9
1998 [3]................	131,463	108,202	23,261	82.3	17.7
1999 [3]................	133,488	110,302	23,186	82.6	17.4
2000 [3]................	136,891	113,846	23,044	83.2	16.8
2001................	136,933	113,573	23,361	82.9	17.1
2002................	136,485	112,700	23,785	82.6	17.4
2003 [3]................	137,736	113,324	24,412	82.3	17.7
2004	139,252	114,518	24,734	82.2	17.8
2005	141,730	117,016	24,714	82.6	17.4
2006	144,427	119,688	24,739	82.9	17.1
2007	146,047	121,091	24,956	82.9	17.1
2008 [3]................	145,362	120,030	25,332	82.6	17.4

See footnotes at end of table.

Table 20. **Employed persons by full- and part-time status and sex, 1970-2008 annual averages—Continued**

(Numbers in thousands)

Year	Women				
	Total employed	Usually full time [1]	Usually part time [2]	Percent usually full time	Percent usually part time
1970................	29,688	21,929	7,758	73.9	26.1
1971................	29,976	21,950	8,026	73.2	26.8
1972 [3]...........	31,257	22,842	8,416	73.1	26.9
1973 [3]...........	32,715	23,960	8,756	73.2	26.8
1974................	33,769	24,714	9,055	73.2	26.8
1975................	33,989	24,598	9,391	72.4	27.6
1976................	35,615	25,814	9,799	72.5	27.5
1977................	37,289	27,076	10,213	72.6	27.4
1978 [3]...........	39,569	28,912	10,658	73.1	26.9
1979................	41,217	30,227	10,990	73.3	26.7
1980................	42,117	30,845	11,270	73.2	26.8
1981................	43,000	31,337	11,664	72.9	27.1
1982................	43,256	31,086	12,170	71.9	28.1
1983................	44,047	31,679	12,367	71.9	28.1
1984................	45,915	33,473	12,441	72.9	27.1
1985................	47,259	34,672	12,587	73.4	26.6
1986 [3]...........	48,706	35,845	12,862	73.6	26.4
1987................	50,334	37,210	13,124	73.9	26.1
1988................	51,696	38,398	13,298	74.3	25.7
1989................	53,027	39,484	13,544	74.5	25.5
1990 [3]...........	53,689	40,165	13,524	74.8	25.2
1991................	53,496	39,783	13,713	74.4	25.6
1992................	54,052	40,301	13,751	74.6	25.4
1993................	54,910	40,991	13,919	74.7	25.3
1994 [3]...........	56,610	40,940	15,670	72.3	27.7
1995................	57,523	41,743	15,779	72.6	27.4
1996................	58,501	42,776	15,725	73.1	26.9
1997 [3]...........	59,873	44,076	15,797	73.6	26.4
1998 [3]...........	60,771	45,014	15,757	74.1	25.9
1999 [3]...........	62,042	46,372	15,670	74.7	25.3
2000 [3]...........	63,586	47,916	15,670	75.4	24.6
2001................	63,737	47,950	15,788	75.2	24.8
2002................	63,582	47,494	16,088	74.7	25.3
2003 [3]...........	64,404	47,946	16,459	74.4	25.6
2004	64,728	48,073	16,654	74.3	25.7
2005	65,757	49,158	16,598	74.8	25.2
2006	66,925	50,380	16,545	75.3	24.7
2007	67,792	51,056	16,736	75.3	24.7
2008 [3]...........	67,876	51,178	16,698	75.4	24.6

See footnotes at end of table.

Table 20. **Employed persons by full- and part-time status and sex, 1970-2008 annual averages—Continued**

(Numbers in thousands)

Year	Men				
	Total employed	Usually full time [1]	Usually part time [2]	Percent usually full time	Percent usually part time
1970..............	48,990	44,825	4,166	91.5	8.5
1971..............	49,390	45,023	4,367	91.2	8.8
1972 [3]............	50,896	46,373	4,523	91.1	8.9
1973 [3]............	52,349	47,843	4,507	91.4	8.6
1974..............	53,024	48,378	4,646	91.2	8.8
1975..............	51,857	46,988	4,870	90.6	9.4
1976..............	53,138	48,150	4,988	90.6	9.4
1977..............	54,728	49,551	5,178	90.5	9.5
1978 [3]............	56,479	51,281	5,198	90.8	9.2
1979..............	57,607	52,427	5,180	91.0	9.0
1980..............	57,186	51,717	5,471	90.4	9.6
1981..............	57,397	51,906	5,492	90.4	9.6
1982..............	56,271	50,334	5,937	89.4	10.6
1983..............	56,787	50,643	6,145	89.2	10.8
1984..............	59,091	53,070	6,020	89.8	10.2
1985..............	59,891	53,862	6,028	89.9	10.1
1986 [3]............	60,892	54,685	6,207	89.8	10.2
1987..............	62,107	55,746	6,360	89.8	10.2
1988..............	63,273	56,816	6,457	89.8	10.2
1989..............	64,315	57,885	6,430	90.0	10.0
1990 [3]............	65,104	58,501	6,604	89.9	10.1
1991..............	64,223	57,407	6,815	89.4	10.6
1992..............	64,440	57,363	7,077	89.0	11.0
1993..............	65,349	58,123	7,226	88.9	11.1
1994 [3]............	66,450	58,832	7,617	88.5	11.5
1995..............	67,377	59,936	7,441	89.0	11.0
1996..............	68,207	60,762	7,445	89.1	10.9
1997 [3]............	69,685	62,258	7,427	89.3	10.7
1998 [3]............	70,693	63,189	7,504	89.4	10.6
1999 [3]............	71,446	63,930	7,516	89.5	10.5

See footnotes at end of table.

Table 20. **Employed persons by full- and part-time status and sex, 1970-2008 annual averages—Continued**

(Numbers in thousands)

Year	Men				
	Total employed	Usually full time [1]	Usually part time [2]	Percent usually full time	Percent usually part time
2000 [3]	73,305	65,930	7,375	89.9	10.1
2001..............	73,196	65,623	7,573	89.7	10.3
2002..............	72,903	65,205	7,697	89.4	10.6
2003 [3]	73,332	65,379	7,953	89.2	10.8
2004	74,524	66,444	8,080	89.2	10.8
2005	75,973	67,858	8,115	89.3	10.7
2006	77,502	69,307	8,194	89.4	10.6
2007	78,254	70,035	8,220	89.5	10.5
2008 [3]	77,486	68,853	8,634	88.9	11.1

[1] Prior to 1994, total includes persons who usually work part-time but who worked 35 or more hours during the reference week; for 1994 and later years, such persons were included in the part-time total. In all years, the total includes those who usually work full time but who worked less than 35 hours during the reference week for noneconomic reasons, such as illness or holiday, and those absent from work for the entire reference week who usually work full time. These groups are not shown separately.

[2] For all years, total includes those who usually work less than 35 hours a week but who were absent from work for the entire reference week and for 1994 and later years, those who worked 35 or more hours during the reference week. These groups are not shown separately.

[3] The comparability of historical labor force data has been affected at various times by methodological and conceptual changes in the Current Population Survey (CPS). For an explanation, see the Historical Comparability documentation provided at **http://www.bls.gov/cps/eetech_methods.pdf** .

SOURCE: Current Population Survey, U.S. Department of Labor, U.S. Bureau of Labor Statistics.

Table 21. **Average weekly hours at work in all industries and in nonagricultural industries by sex, 1976-2008 annual averages**

Year	All industries			Nonagricultural industries		
	Total	Women	Men	Total	Women	Men
1976.......	38.7	34.1	41.7	38.4	34.1	41.4
1977.......	38.8	34.2	41.9	38.5	34.2	41.6
1978 [1].....	39.0	34.5	42.1	38.7	34.4	41.8
1979.......	38.9	34.5	42.0	38.6	34.4	41.7
1980.......	38.5	34.5	41.5	38.3	34.4	41.2
1981.......	38.1	34.1	41.1	37.9	34.1	40.7
1982.......	38.0	34.1	40.9	37.7	34.0	40.6
1983.......	38.3	34.5	41.2	38.1	34.4	41.0
1984.......	38.8	34.9	41.8	38.6	34.9	41.5
1985.......	39.0	35.2	42.0	38.9	35.2	41.8
1986 [1].....	39.1	35.4	42.1	38.9	35.3	41.9
1987.......	39.0	35.3	42.0	38.8	35.3	41.8
1988.......	39.4	35.7	42.4	39.3	35.7	42.2
1989.......	39.6	35.8	42.6	39.4	35.8	42.4
1990 [1].....	39.4	35.8	42.3	39.3	35.8	42.1
1991.......	39.2	35.8	42.0	39.1	35.8	41.9
1992.......	38.9	35.6	41.7	38.8	35.6	41.6
1993.......	39.4	36.0	42.2	39.3	36.0	42.1
1994 [1].....	39.2	35.5	42.2	39.1	35.6	42.1
1995.......	39.3	35.6	42.3	39.2	35.7	42.2
1996.......	39.3	35.7	42.3	39.2	35.7	42.2
1997 [1].....	39.5	36.0	42.4	39.4	36.0	42.3
1998 [1].....	39.3	35.8	42.2	39.2	35.9	42.2
1999 [1].....	39.6	36.2	42.4	39.5	36.2	42.4
2000 [1].....	39.7	36.4	42.5	39.6	36.4	42.4
2001.......	39.2	36.1	41.9	39.2	36.1	41.8
2002.......	39.2	36.0	41.8	39.1	36.1	41.7
2003 [1].....	39.0	35.9	41.7	39.0	35.9	41.6
2004.......	39.0	35.9	41.7	39.0	35.9	41.6
2005.......	39.2	36.1	41.8	39.1	36.1	41.7
2006.......	39.2	36.2	41.8	39.2	36.2	41.7
2007.......	39.2	36.1	41.7	39.1	36.1	41.6
2008 [1].....	38.9	36.1	41.3	38.8	36.1	41.2

[1] The comparability of historical data has been affected at various times by methodological and conceptual changes in the Current Population Survey (CPS). For an explanation, see the Historical Comparability documentation provided at **http://www.bls.gov/cps/eetech_methods.pdf**.

SOURCE: Current Population Survey, U.S. Department of Labor, U.S. Bureau of Labor Statistics.

Table 22. **Work experience of the population by sex and full- and part-time status, selected years, 1970-2007**

(Percent distribution)

Year	Population (in thousands)	With work experience		Percent distribution by work experience						
		Total (in thousands)	Percent of population	Total	Usually work full time			Usually work part time		
					Total	50 to 52 weeks	1 to 49 weeks	Total	50 to 52 weeks	1 to 49 weeks
Total, both sexes										
1970...................	138,953	93,850	67.5	100.0	79.4	55.6	23.8	20.6	6.7	13.9
1975...................	153,180	102,603	67.0	100.0	78.9	54.3	24.6	21.2	7.5	13.7
1980...................	169,452	115,752	68.3	100.0	78.5	56.1	22.4	21.4	7.7	13.7
1985...................	179,944	123,466	68.6	100.0	78.2	58.7	19.5	21.9	8.3	13.6
1990 [1]...............	189,238	132,562	70.1	100.0	78.8	60.4	18.4	21.3	8.7	12.6
1995...................	199,925	138,971	69.5	100.0	78.6	62.9	15.7	21.3	9.1	12.2
2000 [1]...............	214,292	150,787	70.4	100.0	80.4	66.7	13.7	19.5	9.3	10.2
2005...................	227,975	154,322	67.7	100.0	80.3	67.5	12.8	19.7	10.0	9.7
2006...................	231,033	156,658	67.8	100.0	80.9	68.4	12.5	19.1	9.7	9.4
2007...................	232,995	157,653	67.7	100.0	80.9	68.4	12.5	19.1	9.8	9.3
Women										
1970...................	73,657	38,809	52.7	100.0	67.9	40.7	27.2	32.2	10.1	22.1
1975...................	80,834	43,511	53.8	100.0	67.1	41.4	25.7	32.8	11.7	21.1
1980...................	89,259	51,492	57.7	100.0	67.7	44.7	23.0	32.3	11.9	20.4
1985...................	94,490	56,165	59.4	100.0	68.1	48.9	19.2	31.8	12.3	19.5
1990 [1]...............	98,970	61,494	62.1	100.0	69.8	51.5	18.3	30.2	12.8	17.4
1995...................	104,058	65,304	62.8	100.0	70.2	54.3	15.9	29.7	13.3	16.4
2000 [1]...............	111,440	71,341	64.0	100.0	72.9	58.4	14.5	27.1	13.4	13.7
2005...................	117,814	72,309	61.4	100.0	72.7	59.9	12.8	27.3	14.1	13.2
2006...................	119,300	73,527	61.6	100.0	73.0	60.7	12.3	27.0	14.1	12.9
2007...................	120,300	74,115	61.6	100.0	73.6	61.5	12.1	26.4	14.2	12.2
Men										
1970...................	65,296	55,041	84.3	100.0	87.6	66.1	21.5	12.4	4.4	8.0
1975...................	72,346	59,091	81.7	100.0	87.5	63.8	23.7	12.5	4.4	8.1
1980...................	80,193	64,260	80.1	100.0	87.2	65.2	22.0	12.8	4.4	8.4
1985...................	85,454	67,301	78.8	100.0	86.5	66.8	19.7	13.5	4.8	8.7
1990 [1]...............	90,269	71,068	78.7	100.0	86.4	68.0	18.4	13.5	5.1	8.4
1995...................	95,867	73,667	76.8	100.0	86.2	70.6	15.6	13.9	5.5	8.4
2000 [1]...............	102,853	79,446	77.2	100.0	87.5	74.2	13.3	12.6	5.5	7.1
2005...................	110,161	82,013	74.4	100.0	87.0	74.2	12.8	13.0	6.3	6.7
2006...................	111,733	83,131	74.4	100.0	87.8	75.2	12.6	12.2	5.7	6.5
2007...................	112,695	83,538	74.1	100.0	87.4	74.6	12.8	12.6	5.9	6.7

[1] The comparability of historical labor force data has been affected at various times by methodological and conceptual changes in the Current Population Survey (CPS). For an explanation, see the Historical Comparability documentation provided at **http://www.bls.gov/cps/eetech_methods.pdf**.

NOTE: These data, collected in the Annual Social and Economic Supplement, reflect the work experience of the entire year.

SOURCE: Annual Social and Economic Supplements, 1971-2008, Current Population Survey, U.S. Department of Labor, U.S. Bureau of Labor Statistics.

Table 23. Married-couple families by number and relationship of earners, 1967-2007

(Numbers in thousands)

Year	Married-couple families										
	Total	No earners	One earner				Two earners or more				
			Total	Husband only	Wife only	Other family member	Total	Husband and wife	Husband and other family member	Wife and other family member	Husband and wife are not earners
1967	43,292	2,943	16,490	15,429	716	345	23,859	18,888	4,639	-	-
1968	43,842	2,888	16,375	15,310	730	335	24,579	19,743	4,522	-	-
1969	44,436	3,022	16,268	15,133	797	339	25,145	20,327	4,517	-	-
1970	44,832	3,252	16,117	14,931	867	320	25,464	20,510	4,622	-	-
1971	45,939	3,471	16,847	15,502	1,004	340	25,621	20,641	4,651	-	-
1972	46,594	3,632	16,787	15,387	1,003	398	26,175	21,279	4,553	-	-
1973	47,185	4,027	16,080	14,547	1,110	423	27,078	22,152	4,535	-	-
1974	47,438	4,325	15,795	14,122	1,216	457	27,319	22,451	4,442	-	-
1975	47,878	4,943	16,217	14,343	1,394	481	26,717	22,338	3,861	-	-
1976	48,150	4,962	15,630	13,690	1,424	516	27,559	23,104	3,829	-	-
1977	48,131	5,177	15,119	13,153	1,456	512	27,835	23,474	3,812	-	-
1978	48,532	5,226	14,456	12,434	1,509	513	28,850	24,655	3,609	-	-
1979	49,132	5,559	13,912	11,934	1,499	480	29,660	25,595	3,476	-	-
1980	49,316	5,903	13,900	11,621	1,707	573	29,513	25,557	3,380	-	-
1981	49,669	6,213	13,832	11,524	1,680	628	29,624	25,729	3,212	-	-
1982	49,947	6,427	14,235	11,575	2,048	613	29,285	25,387	3,149	-	-
1983	50,134	6,549	13,692	11,100	1,944	647	29,893	26,119	2,996	-	-
1984	50,395	6,630	12,952	10,472	1,852	628	30,814	27,035	2,891	-	-
1985	50,978	6,693	12,961	10,406	1,897	658	31,324	27,787	2,764	-	-
1986	51,574	6,731	12,565	9,984	1,917	664	32,278	28,811	2,730	-	-
1987	51,847	6,741	12,435	9,787	1,946	702	32,671	29,369	2,576	-	-
1988	52,149	6,754	11,876	9,463	1,777	636	33,519	30,536	2,303	532	148
1989	52,385	6,812	11,748	9,212	1,840	695	33,825	30,879	2,373	435	138
1990	52,241	6,770	11,630	9,107	1,826	698	33,841	30,829	2,369	479	164
1991	52,549	7,091	11,523	8,873	1,993	657	33,935	31,049	2,161	527	197
1992	53,254	7,256	11,977	9,114	2,145	718	34,021	31,268	1,940	624	189
1993	53,248	7,282	11,842	8,745	2,411	687	34,123	31,302	2,051	614	156
1994	53,929	7,227	11,774	8,719	2,374	681	34,928	32,125	2,048	603	151
1995	53,621	7,278	11,739	8,821	2,253	664	34,604	32,061	1,878	539	127
1996	53,654	7,148	11,556	8,671	2,214	671	34,950	32,406	1,899	522	123
1997	54,362	7,289	11,728	8,792	2,302	634	35,345	32,764	1,853	569	158
1998	54,829	7,257	12,279	9,198	2,419	662	35,293	32,810	1,726	616	141
1999	55,352	7,163	12,328	9,093	2,595	640	35,861	33,360	1,815	519	167
2000	56,643	7,463	12,717	9,515	2,601	600	36,463	33,892	1,865	566	139
2001	56,798	7,666	12,907	9,621	2,698	588	36,224	33,696	1,898	501	129
2002	57,362	7,803	13,487	10,109	2,818	560	36,071	33,547	1,845	558	121
2003	57,767	8,043	14,051	10,469	3,026	557	35,673	33,220	1,789	548	117
2004	58,045	7,996	14,352	10,821	2,991	540	35,696	33,131	1,832	610	123
2005	58,225	8,017	14,292	10,603	3,096	593	35,915	33,380	1,818	597	121
2006	59,050	8,091	14,545	10,693	3,261	591	36,414	33,880	1,752	639	142
2007	58,490	7,914	14,264	10,392	3,265	608	36,312	33,718	1,847	597	149

See note at end of table.

Table 23. **Married-couple families by number and relationship of earners, 1967-2007—Continued**

(Percent distribution)

Year	Married-couple families										
			One earner				Two earners or more				
	Total	No earners	Total	Husband only	Wife only	Other family member	Total	Husband and wife	Husband and other family member	Wife and other family member	Husband and wife are not earners
1967.......	100.0	6.8	38.1	35.6	1.7	0.8	55.1	43.6	10.7	-	-
1968.......	100.0	6.6	37.4	34.9	1.7	.8	56.1	45.0	10.3	-	-
1969.......	100.0	6.8	36.6	34.1	1.8	.8	56.6	45.7	10.2	-	-
1970.......	100.0	7.3	35.9	33.3	1.9	.7	56.8	45.7	10.3	-	-
1971.......	100.0	7.6	36.7	33.7	2.2	.7	55.8	44.9	10.1	-	-
1972.......	100.0	7.8	36.0	33.0	2.2	.9	56.2	45.7	9.8	-	-
1973.......	100.0	8.5	34.1	30.8	2.4	.9	57.4	46.9	9.6	-	-
1974.......	100.0	9.1	33.3	29.8	2.6	1.0	57.6	47.3	9.4	-	-
1975.......	100.0	10.3	33.9	30.0	2.9	1.0	55.8	46.7	8.1	-	-
1976.......	100.0	10.3	32.5	28.4	3.0	1.1	57.2	48.0	8.0	-	-
1977.......	100.0	10.8	31.4	27.3	3.0	1.1	57.8	48.8	7.9	-	-
1978.......	100.0	10.8	29.8	25.6	3.1	1.1	59.4	50.8	7.4	-	-
1979.......	100.0	11.3	28.3	24.3	3.1	1.0	60.4	52.1	7.1	-	-
1980.......	100.0	12.0	28.2	23.6	3.5	1.2	59.8	51.8	6.9	-	-
1981.......	100.0	12.5	27.8	23.2	3.4	1.3	59.6	51.8	6.5	-	-
1982.......	100.0	12.9	28.5	23.2	4.1	1.2	58.6	50.8	6.3	-	-
1983.......	100.0	13.1	27.3	22.1	3.9	1.3	59.6	52.1	6.0	-	-
1984.......	100.0	13.2	25.7	20.8	3.7	1.2	61.1	53.6	5.7	-	-
1985.......	100.0	13.1	25.4	20.4	3.7	1.3	61.4	54.5	5.4	-	-
1986.......	100.0	13.1	24.4	19.4	3.7	1.3	62.6	55.9	5.3	-	-
1987.......	100.0	13.0	24.0	18.9	3.8	1.4	63.0	56.6	5.0	-	-
1988.......	100.0	13.0	22.8	18.1	3.4	1.2	64.3	58.6	4.4	1.0	0.3
1989.......	100.0	13.0	22.4	17.6	3.5	1.3	64.6	58.9	4.5	.8	.3
1990.......	100.0	13.0	22.3	17.4	3.5	1.3	64.8	59.0	4.5	.9	.3
1991.......	100.0	13.5	21.9	16.9	3.8	1.3	64.6	59.1	4.1	1.0	.4
1992.......	100.0	13.6	22.5	17.1	4.0	1.3	63.9	58.7	3.6	1.2	.4
1993.......	100.0	13.7	22.2	16.4	4.5	1.3	64.1	58.8	3.9	1.2	.3
1994.......	100.0	13.4	21.8	16.2	4.4	1.3	64.8	59.6	3.8	1.1	.3
1995.......	100.0	13.6	21.9	16.5	4.2	1.2	64.5	59.8	3.5	1.0	.2
1996.......	100.0	13.3	21.5	16.2	4.1	1.3	65.1	60.4	3.5	1.0	.2
1997.......	100.0	13.4	21.6	16.2	4.2	1.2	65.0	60.3	3.4	1.0	.3
1998.......	100.0	13.2	22.4	16.8	4.4	1.2	64.4	59.8	3.1	1.1	.3
1999.......	100.0	12.9	22.3	16.4	4.7	1.2	64.8	60.3	3.3	.9	.3
2000.......	100.0	13.2	22.5	16.8	4.6	1.1	64.4	59.8	3.3	1.0	.2
2001.......	100.0	13.5	22.7	16.9	4.8	1.0	63.8	59.3	3.3	.9	.2
2002.......	100.0	13.6	23.5	17.6	4.9	1.0	62.9	58.5	3.2	1.0	.2
2003.......	100.0	13.9	24.3	18.1	5.2	1.0	61.8	57.5	3.1	.9	.2
2004.......	100.0	13.8	24.7	18.6	5.2	.9	61.5	57.1	3.2	1.0	.2
2005.......	100.0	13.8	24.5	18.2	5.3	1.0	61.7	57.3	3.1	1.0	.2
2006.......	100.0	13.7	24.6	18.1	5.5	1.0	61.7	57.4	3.0	1.1	.2
2007.......	100.0	13.5	24.4	17.8	5.6	1.0	62.1	57.6	3.2	1.0	.3

NOTE: These data, collected in the Annual Social and Economic Supplement, reflect the earnings and work experience of the entire year. Dash indicates data not available.

SOURCE: Annual Social and Economic Supplements, 1968-2008, Current Population Survey, U.S. Department of Labor, U.S. Bureau of Labor Statistics.

Table 24. **Contribution of wives' earnings to family income, 1970-2007**

Year	Contribution to family income (median percent)
1970	26.6
1971	27.5
1972	26.7
1973	26.0
1974	25.4
1975	26.3
1976	26.4
1977	26.1
1978	26.1
1979	26.0
1980	26.7
1981	27.3
1982	28.4
1983	28.8
1984	28.4
1985	28.3
1986	29.0
1987	29.5
1988	29.6
1989	29.9
1990	30.7
1991	31.3
1992	32.4
1993	32.2
1994	31.9
1995	31.9
1996	32.6
1997	32.7
1998	32.8
1999	32.8
2000	33.5
2001	34.4
2002	34.8
2003	35.2
2004	34.9
2005	35.1
2006	35.6
2007	36.0

NOTE: These data, collected in the Annual Social and Economic Supplement, reflect the earnings and work experience of the entire year.

SOURCE: Annual Social and Economic Supplements, 1971-2008, Current Population Survey, U.S. Department of Labor, U.S. Bureau of Labor Statistics.

Table 25. **Wives who earn more than their husbands, 1987-2007**

(Numbers in thousands)

Year	Families in which wives have earnings but husbands may not			Families in which both wives and husbands have earnings		
	Married-couple families in which wife (but not necessarily husband) had earnings from work	Wives who earn more than their husbands [1]	Percent of wives who earn more than their husbands [1]	Married-couple families in which both wife and husband had earnings from work	Wives who earn more than their husbands [2]	Percent of wives who earn more than their husbands [2]
1987.................	32,025	7,581	23.7	29,755	5,311	17.8
1988.................	32,810	7,827	23.9	30,503	5,520	18.1
1989.................	33,119	8,068	24.4	30,848	5,796	18.8
1990.................	33,093	8,221	24.8	30,794	5,923	19.2
1991.................	33,516	8,983	26.8	30,998	6,465	20.9
1992.................	33,987	9,715	28.6	31,221	6,948	22.3
1993.................	34,286	10,000	29.2	31,264	6,978	22.3
1994.................	35,066	10,184	29.0	32,091	7,209	22.5
1995.................	34,819	9,822	28.2	32,030	7,033	22.0
1996.................	35,120	10,070	28.7	32,389	7,340	22.7
1997.................	35,613	10,309	28.9	32,745	7,441	22.7
1998.................	35,806	10,467	29.2	32,782	7,443	22.7
1999.................	36,454	10,548	28.9	33,340	7,434	22.3
2000.................	37,037	11,070	29.9	33,873	7,906	23.3
2001.................	36,864	11,329	30.7	33,665	8,130	24.1
2002.................	36,905	11,765	31.9	33,531	8,391	25.0
2003.................	36,761	11,923	32.4	33,189	8,351	25.2
2004.................	36,710	11,985	32.6	33,110	8,386	25.3
2005.................	37,055	12,215	33.0	33,364	8,524	25.5
2006.................	37,733	12,601	33.4	33,838	8,707	25.7
2007.................	37,536	12,570	33.5	33,678	8,712	25.9

[1] Includes families in which husband had no earnings from work.

[2] Excludes families in which husband had no earnings from work.

NOTE: These data, collected in the Annual Social and Economic Supplement, reflect the earnings and work experience of the entire year.

SOURCE: Annual Social and Economic Supplements, 1988-2008, Current Population Survey, U.S. Department of Labor, U.S. Bureau of Labor Statistics.

Table 26. **Wage and salary workers paid hourly rates with earnings at or below the prevailing Federal minimum wage by selected characteristics, 2008 annual averages**

(Numbers in thousands)

Characteristic	Workers paid hourly rates				
	Total	Total at or below prevailing Federal minimum wage			
		Total	Percent of hourly paid workers	At prevailing Federal minimum wage	Below prevailing Federal minimum wage
Age and sex					
Total, 16 years and over.................................	75,305	2,226	3.0	286	1,940
16 to 24 years...	15,680	1,122	7.2	161	961
25 years and over......................................	59,626	1,104	1.9	125	979
Women, 16 years and over...............................	37,972	1,498	3.9	196	1,302
16 to 24 years...	7,701	738	9.6	103	635
25 years and over......................................	30,270	759	2.5	93	666
Men, 16 years and over.................................	37,334	728	1.9	90	638
16 to 24 years...	7,978	384	4.8	58	326
25 years and over......................................	29,356	345	1.2	32	313
Race and Hispanic or Latino ethnicity					
White..	60,464	1,783	2.9	215	1,568
Women...	29,931	1,224	4.1	151	1,073
Men...	30,533	560	1.8	65	495
Black or African American..............................	9,866	308	3.1	49	259
Women...	5,457	186	3.4	32	154
Men...	4,408	122	2.8	17	105
Asian..	2,844	69	2.4	11	58
Women...	1,543	42	2.7	8	34
Men...	1,301	27	2.1	3	24
Hispanic or Latino	13,070	324	2.5	39	285
Women...	5,313	191	3.6	23	168
Men...	7,756	132	1.7	15	117

Table 26. **Wage and salary workers paid hourly rates with earnings at or below the prevailing Federal minimum wage by selected characteristics, 2008 annual averages—Continued**

(Numbers in thousands)

Characteristic	Total	Workers paid hourly rates			
		Total at or below prevailing Federal minimum wage			
		Total	Percent of hourly paid workers	At prevailing Federal minimum wage	Below prevailing Federal minimum wage
Full- and part-time status [1]					
Full-time workers................................	56,837	873	1.5	95	778
Women................................	25,474	532	2.1	68	464
Men................................	31,363	340	1.1	27	313
Part-time workers................................	18,334	1,353	7.4	191	1,162
Women................................	12,431	965	7.8	128	837
Men................................	5,903	388	6.6	63	325

[1] The distinction between full- and part-time workers is based on hours usually worked. These data will not sum to totals because full- or part-time status on the principal job is not identifiable for a small number of multiple jobholders.

NOTE: The prevailing Federal minimum wage rose from $5.85 to $6.55 an hour on July 24, 2008. Data in this table reflect the average number of workers who earned $5.85 or less from January 2008 through July 2008 and those who earned $6.55 or less from August 2008 through the end of the year. Data are for wage and salary workers, excluding the incorporated self-employed. They refer to a person's earnings on his or her sole or principal job, and pertain only to workers who are paid hourly rates. Salaried workers and other nonhourly workers are not included. Estimates for the above race groups (white, black or African American, and Asian) do not sum to totals because data are not presented for all races. Persons whose ethnicity is identified as Hispanic or Latino may be of any race.

SOURCE: Current Population Survey, U.S. Department of Labor, U.S. Bureau of Labor Statistics.

Table 27. **Working poor: Poverty status of persons in the labor force for 27 weeks or more by age, sex, race, and Hispanic or Latino ethnicity, 2007**

(Numbers in thousands)

Age and sex	Total					Below poverty level				
	Total	White	Black or African American	Asian	Hispanic or Latino ethnicity	Total	White	Black or African American	Asian	Hispanic or Latino ethnicity
Total, 16 years and older......	146,567	119,792	16,586	6,766	20,461	7,521	5,357	1,612	262	2,139
16 to 19 years...............	4,079	3,397	416	94	664	416	318	71	9	99
20 to 24 years...............	13,315	10,736	1,694	433	2,346	1,413	1,038	296	20	302
25 to 34 years...............	31,963	25,377	3,973	1,698	6,204	2,126	1,460	514	65	713
35 to 44 years...............	34,211	27,346	4,165	1,892	5,458	1,716	1,212	381	67	595
45 to 54 years...............	35,187	29,060	3,885	1,577	3,684	1,175	869	211	55	312
55 to 64 years...............	21,658	18,476	1,982	860	1,682	569	385	117	44	102
65 years and older.........	6,155	5,401	471	212	422	106	75	24	3	16
Women, 16 years and older.	67,624	53,999	8,902	3,167	7,997	3,890	2,592	1,036	123	856
16 to 19 years...............	2,032	1,679	235	39	262	212	162	38	1	42
20 to 24 years...............	6,147	4,919	833	209	893	828	600	187	15	133
25 to 34 years...............	14,428	11,067	2,155	791	2,225	1,125	676	367	37	251
35 to 44 years...............	15,560	12,070	2,259	858	2,171	840	554	228	30	255
45 to 54 years...............	16,502	13,367	2,057	756	1,559	539	379	119	22	122
55 to 64 years...............	10,221	8,539	1,112	416	730	290	183	79	16	47
65 years and older.........	2,734	2,359	251	98	158	55	37	16	1	5
Men, 16 years and older......	78,944	65,794	7,684	3,599	12,464	3,631	2,765	576	140	1,283
16 to 19 years...............	2,048	1,718	181	54	402	204	156	33	7	57
20 to 24 years...............	7,168	5,817	861	224	1,453	584	438	108	4	169
25 to 34 years...............	17,535	14,310	1,818	907	3,978	1,001	783	147	28	462
35 to 44 years...............	18,651	15,276	1,906	1,035	3,288	876	658	152	37	340
45 to 54 years...............	18,685	15,693	1,828	821	2,126	637	490	91	33	190
55 to 64 years...............	11,437	9,937	870	445	953	278	202	38	28	55
65 years and older	3,421	3,042	220	114	264	51	38	7	2	11

Table 27. **Working poor: Poverty status of persons in the labor force for 27 weeks or more by age, sex, race, and Hispanic or Latino ethnicity, 2007—Continued**

Age and sex	Rate [1]				
	Total	White	Black or African American	Asian	Hispanic or Latino ethnicity
Total, 16 years and older......	5.1	4.5	9.7	3.9	10.5
16 to 19 years..............	10.2	9.4	17.0	9.2	14.9
20 to 24 years..............	10.6	9.7	17.4	4.5	12.9
25 to 34 years..............	6.7	5.8	12.9	3.8	11.5
35 to 44 years..............	5.0	4.4	9.1	3.5	10.9
45 to 54 years..............	3.3	3.0	5.4	3.5	8.5
55 to 64 years..............	2.6	2.1	5.9	5.1	6.1
65 years and older........	1.7	1.4	5.0	1.3	3.7
Women, 16 years and older.	5.8	4.8	11.6	3.9	10.7
16 to 19 years..............	10.4	9.7	16.3	([2])	16.1
20 to 24 years..............	13.5	12.2	22.5	7.3	14.9
25 to 34 years..............	7.8	6.1	17.0	4.7	11.3
35 to 44 years..............	5.4	4.6	10.1	3.5	11.8
45 to 54 years..............	3.3	2.8	5.8	2.9	7.8
55 to 64 years..............	2.8	2.1	7.1	3.9	6.4
65 years and older........	2.0	1.6	6.5	.6	3.2
Men, 16 years and older......	4.6	4.2	7.5	3.9	10.3
16 to 19 years..............	10.0	9.1	18.0	([2])	14.1
20 to 24 years..............	8.2	7.5	12.6	2.0	11.6
25 to 34 years..............	5.7	5.5	8.1	3.1	11.6
35 to 44 years..............	4.7	4.3	8.0	3.5	10.3
45 to 54 years..............	3.4	3.1	5.0	4.0	8.9
55 to 64 years..............	2.4	2.0	4.3	6.2	5.8
65 years and older........	1.5	1.3	3.3	1.9	4.0

[1] Number below the poverty level as a percent of the total in the labor force for 27 weeks or more.

[2] Data not shown where labor force base is less than 80,000.

NOTE: These data, collected in the Annual Social and Economic Supplement, reflect the earnings and work experience of the entire year. Estimates for the above race groups (white, black or African American, and Asian) do not sum to totals because data are not presented for all races. Persons whose ethnicity is identified as Hispanic or Latino may be of any race.

SOURCE: 2008 Annual Social and Economic Supplement, Current Population Survey, U.S. Department of Labor, U.S. Bureau of Labor Statistics.

Table 28. **Percent distribution of employed persons by age, sex, and contingent and noncontingent status, February 2005**

Age and sex	Total employed (in thousands)	Contingent workers[1]			Noncontingent workers[1]
		Estimate 1	Estimate 2	Estimate 3	
Total, 16 years and over......	138,952	1.8	2.3	4.1	95.9
16 to 19 years................	5,510	5.6	6.1	8.6	91.4
20 to 24 years................	13,114	4.6	5.2	8.2	91.8
25 to 34 years................	30,103	2.3	2.9	4.8	95.2
35 to 44 years................	34,481	1.2	1.7	3.0	97.0
45 to 54 years................	32,947	.8	1.2	2.7	97.3
55 to 64 years................	17,980	.8	1.1	3.0	97.0
65 years and over............	4,817	1.6	2.3	5.2	94.8
Women, 16 years and over...	65,006	1.8	2.4	4.3	95.7
16 to 19 years................	2,931	5.6	6.2	8.4	91.6
20 to 24 years................	6,186	4.0	4.8	7.8	92.2
25 to 34 years................	13,480	2.2	2.7	4.6	95.4
35 to 44 years................	15,958	1.1	1.7	3.2	96.8
45 to 54 years................	15,754	1.1	1.6	3.2	96.8
55 to 64 years................	8,495	.9	1.1	3.2	96.8
65 years and over............	2,202	2.6	3.5	7.2	92.8
Men, 16 years and over........	73,946	1.8	2.2	3.9	96.1
16 to 19 years................	2,579	5.6	6.1	8.9	91.2
20 to 24 years................	6,928	5.2	5.7	8.6	91.4
25 to 34 years................	16,624	2.4	3.1	5.0	95.0
35 to 44 years................	18,523	1.3	1.6	2.9	97.1
45 to 54 years................	17,193	.6	.8	2.1	97.9
55 to 64 years................	9,485	.7	1.1	2.8	97.2
65 years and over............	2,615	.7	1.3	3.5	96.5

[1] Contingent workers are those who do not have an implicit or explicit contract for ongoing employment. Persons who do not expect to continue in their jobs for personal reasons, such as retirement or returning to school, are not considered contingent workers, provided that they would have the option of continuing in the job were it not for these personal reasons. *Estimate 1* includes wage and salary workers who expect their jobs will last for an additional year or less and who had worked at their jobs for 1 year or less. *Estimate 2* includes wage and salary workers, the self-employed, and independent contractors who expect their employment to last for an additional year or less and who had worked at their jobs (or been self-employed) for 1 year or less. *Estimate 3* includes all workers who do not expect their jobs to last. This is the broadest definition of contingency and estimates 1 and 2 of contingency are included in estimate 3. Noncontingent workers are those workers who do not fall into any of the three definitions of contingency.

SOURCE: Contingent and alternative work arrangements supplement to the Current Population Survey, last conducted in February 2005, U.S. Department of Labor, U.S. Bureau of Labor Statistics.

Table 29. **Percent distribution of employed persons by age, sex, and alternative work arrangements, February 2005**

| Age and sex | Total employed (in thousands) | Total | Percent of workers with alternative arrangements[1] | | | | Workers with traditional arrangements |
			Independent contractors	On-call workers	Temporary help agency workers	Workers provided by contract firms	
Total, 16 years and over......	138,952	100.0	7.4	1.8	0.9	0.6	89.1
16 to 19 years.................	5,510	100.0	1.6	2.4	.6	.1	94.3
20 to 24 years.................	13,114	100.0	2.7	2.7	1.5	.7	91.9
25 to 34 years.................	30,103	100.0	5.0	1.8	1.2	.7	91.1
35 to 44 years.................	34,481	100.0	8.0	1.7	.7	.6	88.9
45 to 54 years.................	32,947	100.0	8.5	1.3	.6	.6	89.0
55 to 64 years.................	17,980	100.0	10.8	1.5	.8	.6	86.2
65 years and over.............	4,817	100.0	18.3	3.6	.7	.4	76.8
Women, 16 years and over...	65,006	100.0	5.6	1.9	1.0	.4	91.0
16 to 19 years.................	2,931	100.0	1.9	1.8	.3	-	95.7
20 to 24 years.................	6,186	100.0	2.6	2.5	1.5	.4	92.5
25 to 34 years.................	13,480	100.0	3.8	1.8	1.3	.5	92.6
35 to 44 years.................	15,958	100.0	5.8	2.0	.8	.4	91.0
45 to 54 years.................	15,754	100.0	6.6	1.3	.8	.3	90.9
55 to 64 years.................	8,495	100.0	7.7	1.9	1.0	.5	88.8
65 years and over.............	2,202	100.0	13.3	3.8	.8	.7	81.1
Men, 16 years and over......	73,946	100.0	9.1	1.7	.8	.8	87.5
16 to 19 years.................	2,579	100.0	1.2	3.2	.9	.3	92.6
20 to 24 years.................	6,928	100.0	2.8	2.9	1.5	.9	91.4
25 to 34 years.................	16,624	100.0	6.1	1.8	1.1	.8	89.9
35 to 44 years.................	18,523	100.0	9.8	1.4	.6	.8	87.1
45 to 54 years.................	17,193	100.0	10.3	1.2	.4	.8	87.3
55 to 64 years.................	9,485	100.0	13.6	1.1	.5	.7	83.9
65 years and over.............	2,615	100.0	22.5	3.5	.6	.1	73.3

[1] *Independent contractors* are workers who were identified as independent contractors, independent consultants, or freelance workers, whether they were self-employed or wage and salary workers. *On-call workers* are workers who are called to work only as needed, although they can be scheduled to work for several days or weeks in a row. *Temporary help agency workers* are workers who were paid by a temporary help agency, whether or not their job was temporary. *Workers provided by contract firms* are workers who are employed by a company that provides them or their services to others under contract and who are usually assigned to only one customer and usually work at the customer's worksite.

NOTE: Workers with traditional arrangements are those who do not fall into any of the "alternative arrangements" categories. Detail may not sum to totals because the total employed includes day laborers (an alternative arrangement, not shown separately) and a small number of workers who were both "on-call" and "provided by contract firms." Dash represents zero.

SOURCE: Contingent and alternative work arrangements supplement to the Current Population Survey, last conducted in February 2005, U.S. Department of Labor, U.S. Bureau of Labor Statistics.

Table 30. **Flexible schedules: Full-time wage and salary workers by selected characteristics, May 2004**

(Numbers in thousands)

Characteristic	Both sexes			Women			Men		
	Total [1]	With flexible schedules [2]		Total [1]	With flexible schedules [2]		Total [1]	With flexible schedules [2]	
		Number	Percent of total		Number	Percent of total		Number	Percent of total
Age									
Total 16 years and over..............	99,778	27,411	27.5	43,366	11,558	26.7	56,412	15,853	28.1
16 to 19 years........................	1,427	336	23.6	524	151	28.9	903	185	20.5
20 years and over....................	98,351	27,075	27.5	42,842	11,406	26.6	55,509	15,668	28.2
20 to 24 years...................	9,004	2,058	22.9	3,856	993	25.8	5,147	1,065	20.7
25 to 34 years...................	24,640	6,902	28.0	10,283	2,851	27.7	14,358	4,051	28.2
35 to 44 years...................	26,766	7,807	29.2	11,342	3,202	28.2	15,424	4,605	29.9
45 to 54 years...................	24,855	6,651	26.8	11,415	2,882	25.2	13,440	3,769	28.0
55 to 64 years...................	11,745	3,181	27.1	5,361	1,316	24.5	6,383	1,865	29.2
65 years and over...............	1,341	475	35.4	585	161	27.6	757	314	41.4
16 to 24 years.......................	10,431	2,394	23.0	4,380	1,144	26.1	6,050	1,250	20.7
25 to 54 years.......................	76,261	21,360	28.0	33,040	8,935	27.0	43,222	12,425	28.7
55 years and over...................	13,086	3,656	27.9	5,946	1,477	24.8	7,140	2,179	30.5
Race and Hispanic or Latino ethnicity									
White...............................	80,498	23,121	28.7	34,276	9,539	27.8	46,222	13,582	29.4
Black or African American........	12,578	2,476	19.7	6,131	1,283	20.9	6,447	1,193	18.5
Asian..............................	4,136	1,132	27.4	1,836	412	22.4	2,300	720	31.3
Hispanic or Latino ethnicity......	14,110	2,596	18.4	5,489	1,166	21.2	8,621	1,430	16.6
Marital status									
Married, spouse present..........	57,630	16,270	28.2	22,704	5,888	25.9	34,926	10,382	29.7
Never married......................	25,144	6,693	26.6	10,676	3,088	28.9	14,469	3,605	24.9
Other marital status...............	17,004	4,448	26.2	9,986	2,582	25.9	7,018	1,866	26.6
Presence and age of children									
With no own children under 18..	61,761	16,759	27.1	27,081	7,349	27.1	34,680	9,410	27.1
With own children under 18......	38,018	10,652	28.0	16,285	4,209	25.8	21,733	6,443	29.6
With own children 6 to 17, none younger.......................	21,739	5,960	27.4	10,262	2,619	25.5	11,477	3,341	29.1
With own children under 6......	16,279	4,692	28.8	6,023	1,590	26.4	10,256	3,102	30.2

[1] Includes persons who did not provide information on flexible schedules.

[2] Persons with flexible schedules are able to vary or make changes in their beginning and ending hours of work, whether or not they have a formal flexitime program on their job.

NOTE: Data relate to the sole or principal job of full-time wage and salary workers who were at work during the survey reference week and exclude all self-employed persons, regardless of whether their businesses were incorporated. Estimates for the above race groups (white, black or African American, and Asian) do not sum to totals because data are not presented for all races. Persons whose ethnicity is identified as Hispanic or Latino may be of any race. Own children include sons, daughters, stepchildren, and adopted children. Not included are nieces, nephews, grandchildren, and other related and unrelated children.

SOURCE: Flexible schedules and shift work supplement to the Current Population Survey, last conducted in May 2004, U.S. Department of Labor, U.S. Bureau of Labor Statistics.

Table 31. **Job-related work at home on primary job: All workers by marital status, presence and age of children, sex, and pay status, May 2004**

(Numbers in thousands)

Characteristic	Total employed [3]	Persons who usually worked at home [1]				
		Total	Rate	Percent distribution by class of worker [2]		
				Wage and salary		Self-employed [4]
				Paid	Unpaid	
Total						
Total, 16 years and over............	136,602	20,673	15.1	16.2	49.3	33.7
Married, spouse present............	77,243	14,623	18.9	16.4	48.1	34.6
Not married............................	59,359	6,050	10.2	15.7	52.2	31.5
Never married......................	36,857	3,087	8.4	17.7	58.1	23.2
Other marital status.............	22,502	2,963	13.2	13.6	46.1	40.2
With own children under 18.......	50,011	8,584	17.2	17.4	47.5	34.0
With own children under 6...	21,373	3,599	16.8	19.2	47.3	32.8
With no own children under 18...	86,591	12,090	14.0	15.4	50.5	33.4
Women						
Total, 16 years and over............	64,185	9,893	15.4	17.8	51.4	29.4
Married, spouse present............	33,750	6,509	19.3	18.2	48.8	31.4
Not married............................	30,435	3,384	11.1	17.1	56.5	25.5
Never married......................	16,754	1,522	9.1	19.2	66.2	12.7
Other marital status.............	13,681	1,862	13.6	15.3	48.6	35.9
With own children under 18.......	24,108	4,051	16.8	19.9	46.6	31.5
With own children under 6...	9,331	1,614	17.3	23.4	42.6	32.6
With no own children under 18...	40,077	5,842	14.6	16.3	54.8	27.9
Men						
Total, 16 years and over............	72,417	10,780	14.9	14.7	47.3	37.6
Married, spouse present............	43,493	8,114	18.7	15.0	47.5	37.1
Not married............................	28,924	2,666	9.2	13.9	46.8	39.1
Never married......................	20,104	1,565	7.8	16.2	50.3	33.3
Other marital status.............	8,820	1,101	12.5	10.5	41.8	47.4
With own children under 18.......	25,903	4,533	17.5	15.1	48.4	36.3
With own children under 6...	12,042	1,986	16.5	15.8	51.0	33.0
With no own children under 18...	46,514	6,247	13.4	14.5	46.5	38.6

[1] Persons who usually work at home are defined as those who work at home at least once per week as part of their primary job.

[2] Unpaid family workers and wage and salary workers who did not report pay status are included in total but not shown separately.

[3] Includes persons who did not provide information on work at home.

[4] Includes both the incorporated and unincorporated self-employed.

NOTE: Data refer to employed persons in nonagricultural industries. Own children include sons, daughters, stepchildren, and adopted children. Not included are nieces, nephews, grandchildren, and other related and unrelated children.

SOURCE: Work at home supplement to the Current Population Survey, last conducted in May 2004, U.S. Department of Labor, U.S. Bureau of Labor Statistics.

Table 32. **Displaced workers[1] by age, sex, race, Hispanic or Latino ethnicity, and employment status in January 2008**

Age, sex, race, and Hispanic or Latino ethnicity	Total (in thousands)	Percent distribution by employment status			
		Total	Employed	Unemployed	Not in labor force
Total					
Total, 20 years and over.............	3,641	100.0	67.1	18.0	15.0
20 to 24 years........................	127	100.0	67.5	22.8	9.7
25 to 54 years........................	2,602	100.0	72.6	17.4	10.0
55 to 64 years........................	708	100.0	60.8	20.7	18.5
65 years and over....................	204	100.0	18.4	12.6	69.0
Women, 20 years and over...........	1,617	100.0	63.5	16.9	19.6
20 to 24 years........................	53	100.0	(^{2})	(^{2})	(^{2})
25 to 54 years........................	1,112	100.0	70.1	15.1	14.8
55 to 64 years........................	352	100.0	53.4	23.6	23.0
65 years and over....................	101	100.0	22.4	9.8	67.8
Men, 20 years and over...............	2,024	100.0	69.9	18.8	11.2
20 to 24 years........................	75	100.0	66.4	22.5	11.1
25 to 54 years........................	1,490	100.0	74.4	19.1	6.5
55 to 64 years........................	356	100.0	68.0	17.9	14.0
65 years and over....................	103	100.0	14.4	15.4	70.2
White					
Total, 20 years and over.............	3,032	100.0	67.9	16.8	15.3
Women.................................	1,348	100.0	64.4	14.9	20.7
Men....................................	1,684	100.0	70.8	18.2	11.0
Black or African American					
Total, 20 years and over.............	408	100.0	58.6	28.2	13.3
Women.................................	187	100.0	56.3	31.1	12.6
Men....................................	221	100.0	60.5	25.7	13.8
Asian					
Total, 20 years and over.............	122	100.0	67.3	11.7	21.0
Women.................................	57	100.0	(^{2})	(^{2})	(^{2})
Men....................................	65	100.0	(^{2})	(^{2})	(^{2})
Hispanic or Latino ethnicity					
Total, 20 years and over.............	423	100.0	68.4	17.4	14.1
Women.................................	153	100.0	65.5	6.9	27.6
Men....................................	270	100.0	70.1	23.4	6.6

[1] Data refer to persons who had 3 or more years of tenure on a job they had lost or left between January 2005 and December 2007 because of plant or company closings or moves, insufficient work, or the abolishment of their positions or shifts.

[2] Data not shown where base is less than 75,000.

NOTE: Estimates for the above race groups (white, black or African American, and Asian) do not sum to totals because data are not presented for all races. Persons whose ethnicity is identified as Hispanic or Latino may be of any race.

SOURCE: January 2008 Displaced Worker supplement to the Current Population Survey, U.S. Department of Labor, U.S. Bureau of Labor Statistics.

Table 33. Labor force status of 2008 high school graduates and 2007-08 high school dropouts 16 to 24 years old by school enrollment and sex, October 2008

(Numbers in thousands)

Characteristic	Civilian noninsti- tutional population	Civilian labor force						Not in labor force
		Total	Percent of population	Employed		Unemployed		
				Total	Percent of population	Total	Percent of labor force	
Total, 2008 high school graduates[1]....	3,151	1,644	52.2	1,310	41.6	334	20.3	1,507
Women..........................	1,511	817	54.1	668	44.2	148	18.2	694
Men.............................	1,640	827	50.4	641	39.1	186	22.5	813
Enrolled in college........................	2,161	888	41.1	756	35.0	132	14.9	1,274
Percent of total 2008 graduates........	68.6	54.0	-	57.7	-	39.5	-	84.5
Women..........................	1,081	499	46.1	428	39.6	70	14.1	583
Percent of female 2008 graduates...	71.5	61.1	-	64.1	-	47.3	-	84.0
Men.............................	1,080	389	36.0	327	30.3	62	15.9	691
Percent of male 2008 graduates......	65.9	47.0	-	51.0	-	33.3	-	85.0
Not enrolled in college......................	989	756	76.4	554	56.0	202	26.7	234
Percent of total 2008 graduates........	31.4	46.0	-	42.3	-	60.5	-	15.5
Women..........................	430	318	74.1	240	55.9	78	24.6	111
Percent of female 2008 graduates...	28.5	38.9	-	35.9	-	52.7	-	16.0
Men.............................	560	438	78.1	314	56.1	124	28.2	122
Percent of male 2008 graduates......	34.1	53.0	-	49.0	-	66.7	-	15.0
Total, 2007-08 high school dropouts[2].	400	194	48.4	117	29.3	77	39.5	206
Women..........................	210	91	43.4	61	29.2	30	32.7	119
Men.............................	191	103	53.9	56	29.3	47	45.6	88

[1] Data refer to persons who graduated from high school between October 2007 and October 2008.

[2] Data refer to persons who dropped out of school between October 2007 and October 2008.

NOTE: Because of rounding, sums of individual items may not equal totals.

SOURCE: October 2008 School Enrollment supplement to the Current Population Survey, U.S. Department of Labor, U.S. Bureau of Labor Statistics.

Table 34. **Labor force status of persons 16 to 24 years old by school enrollment, sex, and educational attainment, October 2008**

(Numbers in thousands)

Characteristic	Civilian noninsti-tutional population	Civilian labor force						Not in labor force
		Total	Percent of population	Employed		Unemployed		
				Total	Percent of population	Total	Percent of labor force	
Enrolled in school.............................	21,348	8,974	42.0	7,907	37.0	1,067	11.9	12,374
Women...	10,865	4,888	45.0	4,426	40.7	463	9.5	5,977
Men...	10,483	4,086	39.0	3,482	33.2	604	14.8	6,397
Enrolled in high school [1]...................	9,677	2,661	27.5	2,099	21.7	562	21.1	7,016
Women...	4,686	1,389	29.6	1,139	24.3	251	18.0	3,297
Men...	4,991	1,272	25.5	960	19.2	311	24.5	3,720
Enrolled in college............................	11,671	6,313	54.1	5,809	49.8	505	8.0	5,358
Women...	6,179	3,499	56.6	3,287	53.2	212	6.1	2,680
Men...	5,492	2,814	51.2	2,522	45.9	293	10.4	2,678
Not enrolled in school....................	16,220	12,957	79.9	11,113	68.5	1,845	14.2	3,263
Women...	7,756	5,728	73.9	5,084	65.6	644	11.2	2,028
Less than a high school diploma	1,403	697	49.6	523	37.2	174	25.0	707
High school graduates, no college [2]	3,200	2,274	71.1	1,982	61.9	292	12.8	926
Some college or associate degree ...	1,953	1,629	83.4	1,525	78.1	104	6.4	324
Bachelor's degree and higher	1,200	1,128	94.1	1,054	87.9	74	6.6	71
Men...	8,465	7,229	85.4	6,028	71.2	1,201	16.6	1,236
Less than a high school diploma	1,606	1,204	74.9	887	55.2	317	26.3	403
High school graduates, no college [2]	4,121	3,487	84.6	2,874	69.7	613	17.6	634
Some college or associate degree ...	1,859	1,696	91.3	1,498	80.6	198	11.7	162
Bachelor's degree and higher	879	842	95.8	769	87.5	73	8.7	37

[1] Includes a small number of persons enrolled in grades below high school.

[2] Includes high school diploma or equivalent.

NOTE: Because of rounding, sums of individual items may not equal totals.

SOURCE: October 2008 School Enrollment supplement to the Current Population Survey, U.S. Department of Labor, U.S. Bureau of Labor Statistics.

Table 35. **Multiple jobholders and multiple jobholding rates by sex and race, May of selected years, 1970-2008, not seasonally adjusted**

(Numbers in thousands)

Year	Total employed	Multiple jobholders				Multiple jobholding rate[1]				
		Total	Women		Men	Total	Women	Men	White	Black or African American [2]
			Number	Percent of all multiple jobholders						
1970......	78,358	4,048	636	15.7	3,412	5.2	2.2	7.0	5.3	4.4
1971......	78,708	4,035	765	19.0	3,270	5.1	2.6	6.7	5.3	3.8
1972......	81,224	3,770	735	19.5	3,035	4.6	2.4	6.0	4.8	3.7
1973......	83,758	4,262	869	20.4	3,393	5.1	2.7	6.6	5.1	4.7
1974......	85,786	3,889	867	22.3	3,022	4.5	2.6	5.8	4.6	3.8
1975......	84,146	3,918	956	24.4	2,962	4.7	2.9	5.8	4.8	3.7
1976......	87,278	3,948	911	23.1	3,037	4.5	2.6	5.8	4.7	2.8
1977......	90,482	4,558	1,241	27.2	3,317	5.0	3.4	6.2	5.3	2.6
1978......	93,904	4,493	1,281	28.5	3,212	4.8	3.3	5.8	5.0	3.1
1979......	96,327	4,724	1,407	29.8	3,317	4.9	3.5	5.9	5.1	3.0
1980......	96,809	4,759	1,549	32.5	3,210	4.9	3.8	5.8	5.1	3.2
1985......	106,878	5,730	2,192	38.3	3,537	5.4	4.7	5.9	5.7	3.2
1989......	117,084	7,225	3,109	43.0	4,115	6.2	5.9	6.4	6.5	4.3
1991......	116,626	7,183	3,129	43.6	4,054	6.2	5.9	6.4	6.4	4.9
1994......	122,946	7,316	3,343	45.7	3,973	6.0	5.9	6.0	6.1	4.9
1995......	124,554	7,952	3,727	46.9	4,225	6.4	6.5	6.3	6.6	5.2
1996......	126,391	7,846	3,494	44.5	4,352	6.2	6.0	6.4	6.4	5.1
1997......	129,565	8,197	3,800	46.4	4,398	6.3	6.4	6.3	6.5	5.7
1998......	131,476	8,126	3,688	45.4	4,438	6.2	6.1	6.3	6.3	5.5
1999......	133,411	7,895	3,778	47.9	4,117	5.9	6.1	5.8	6.0	5.5
2000......	136,685	7,751	3,667	47.3	4,084	5.7	5.8	5.6	5.9	4.9
2001......	137,121	7,540	3,626	48.1	3,914	5.5	5.7	5.3	5.6	5.3
2002......	136,559	7,247	3,511	48.4	3,736	5.3	5.5	5.1	5.5	4.7
2003......	137,567	7,338	3,498	47.7	3,841	5.3	5.4	5.3	5.5	4.3
2004......	138,867	7,258	3,605	49.7	3,653	5.2	5.6	4.9	5.3	5.1
2005......	141,730	6,895	3,402	49.3	3,493	4.9	5.2	4.6	5.4	4.4
2006......	144,041	7,641	3,778	49.4	3,863	5.3	5.7	5.0	5.3	5.4
2007......	145,864	7,693	3,858	50.1	3,835	5.3	5.7	4.9	5.5	4.4
2008......	145,927	7,653	3,812	49.8	3,842	5.2	5.6	4.9	5.4	4.9

[1] Multiple jobholders as a percent of all employed persons in specified group.

[2] Data for years prior to 1977 refer to the black-and-other population group.

NOTE: Data beginning in 1994 are not strictly comparable with data for prior years. For an explanation, see the Historical Comparability documentation provided at **http://www.bls.gov/cps/eetech_methods.pdf.** Comprehensive surveys of multiple jobholders were not conducted in 1981-84, 1986-88, 1990, and 1992-93.

SOURCE: Current Population Survey, U.S. Department of Labor, U.S. Bureau of Labor Statistics.

Table 36. **Unincorporated self-employed persons in nonagricultural industries by sex, 1976-2008 annual averages**

(Numbers in thousands)

Year	Total			Women			Men			Self-employed women as percent of total self-employed
	Total employed	Self-employed	Self-employed as a percent of total	Total employed	Self-employed	Self-employed as a percent of total	Total employed	Self-employed	Self-employed as a percent of total	
1976.....	85,421	5,782	6.8	35,027	1,549	4.4	50,394	4,233	8.4	26.8
1977.....	88,734	6,115	6.9	36,677	1,692	4.6	52,057	4,423	8.5	27.7
1978.....	92,661	6,428	6.9	38,900	1,814	4.7	53,761	4,614	8.6	28.2
1979.....	95,477	6,792	7.1	40,556	1,982	4.9	54,921	4,810	8.8	29.2
1980.....	95,938	7,001	7.3	41,461	2,097	5.1	54,477	4,904	9.0	30.0
1981.....	97,030	7,097	7.3	42,333	2,192	5.2	54,697	4,905	9.0	30.9
1982.....	96,125	7,263	7.6	42,591	2,309	5.4	53,534	4,954	9.3	31.8
1983.....	97,450	7,575	7.8	43,367	2,439	5.6	54,083	5,136	9.5	32.2
1984.....	101,685	7,785	7.7	45,262	2,566	5.7	56,423	5,219	9.2	33.0
1985.....	103,971	7,810	7.5	46,615	2,603	5.6	57,356	5,207	9.1	33.3
1986.....	106,435	7,881	7.4	48,054	2,610	5.4	58,381	5,271	9.0	33.1
1987.....	109,232	8,201	7.5	49,668	2,778	5.6	59,564	5,423	9.1	33.9
1988.....	111,800	8,519	7.6	51,020	2,955	5.8	60,780	5,564	9.2	34.7
1989.....	114,143	8,605	7.5	52,341	3,043	5.8	61,802	5,562	9.0	35.4
1990.....	115,570	8,719	7.5	53,011	3,122	5.9	62,559	5,597	8.9	35.8
1991.....	114,449	8,850	7.7	52,815	3,150	6.0	61,634	5,700	9.2	35.6
1992.....	115,246	8,576	7.4	53,380	2,963	5.6	61,866	5,613	9.1	34.5
1993.....	117,144	8,959	7.6	54,273	3,065	5.6	62,871	5,894	9.4	34.2
1994.....	119,651	9,003	7.5	55,755	3,443	6.2	63,896	5,560	8.7	38.2
1995.....	121,460	8,901	7.3	56,642	3,440	6.1	64,818	5,461	8.4	38.6
1996.....	123,264	8,971	7.3	57,630	3,506	6.1	65,634	5,465	8.3	39.1
1997.....	126,159	9,056	7.2	59,026	3,550	6.0	67,133	5,506	8.2	39.2
1998.....	128,085	8,962	7.0	59,945	3,482	5.8	68,140	5,480	8.0	38.9
1999.....	130,207	8,790	6.8	61,193	3,424	5.6	69,014	5,366	7.8	39.0
2000.....	134,427	9,205	6.8	62,983	3,631	5.8	71,444	5,573	7.8	39.4
2001.....	134,635	9,121	6.8	63,147	3,594	5.7	71,488	5,527	7.7	39.4
2002.....	134,174	8,923	6.7	62,995	3,499	5.6	71,179	5,425	7.6	39.2
2003.....	135,461	9,344	6.9	63,824	3,609	5.7	71,636	5,736	8.0	38.6
2004.....	137,020	9,467	6.9	64,182	3,607	5.6	72,838	5,860	8.0	38.1
2005.....	139,532	9,509	6.8	65,213	3,565	5.5	74,319	5,944	8.0	37.5
2006.....	142,221	9,685	6.8	66,382	3,681	5.5	75,838	6,004	7.9	38.0
2007.....	143,952	9,557	6.6	67,302	3,637	5.4	76,650	5,920	7.7	38.1
2008.....	143,194	9,219	6.4	67,358	3,483	5.2	75,836	5,736	7.6	37.8

NOTE: Beginning in 2000, data reflect the introduction of the 2002 Census industry classification system derived from the 2002 North American Industry Classification System into the Current Population Survey (CPS).

SOURCE: Current Population Survey, U.S. Department of Labor, U.S. Bureau of Labor Statistics.

Table 37. **Employment status of the native-born and foreign-born civilian noninstitutional population by age and sex, 2008 annual averages**

(Numbers in thousands)

Country of birth, age, and sex	Civilian noninsti-tutional population	Civilian labor force						Not in labor force
		Total	Percent of population	Employed		Unemployed		
				Total	Percent of population	Total	Percent of labor force	
Both sexes								
Native born[1]								
16 years and over........	198,471	130,224	65.6	122,703	61.8	7,521	5.8	68,247
16 to 24 years............	33,639	19,821	58.9	17,223	51.2	2,599	13.1	13,818
25 to 34 years............	32,001	27,096	84.7	25,517	79.7	1,579	5.8	4,905
35 to 44 years............	33,372	28,247	84.6	26,984	80.9	1,264	4.5	5,125
45 to 54 years............	37,357	30,623	82.0	29,446	78.8	1,177	3.8	6,734
55 to 64 years............	29,364	18,915	64.4	18,232	62.1	682	3.6	10,450
65 years and over...	32,737	5,522	16.9	5,300	16.2	222	4.0	27,215
Foreign born[2]								
16 years and over........	35,317	24,063	68.1	22,660	64.2	1,403	5.8	11,254
16 to 24 years............	3,845	2,211	57.5	1,979	51.5	232	10.5	1,634
25 to 34 years............	7,992	6,236	78.0	5,866	73.4	371	5.9	1,756
35 to 44 years............	8,327	6,814	81.8	6,473	77.7	341	5.0	1,513
45 to 54 years............	6,602	5,380	81.5	5,083	77.0	297	5.5	1,222
55 to 64 years............	4,126	2,700	65.4	2,580	62.5	120	4.5	1,426
65 years and over... ...	4,424	721	16.3	679	15.3	42	5.9	3,703
Women								
Native born[1]								
16 years and over........	103,047	62,104	60.3	58,795	57.1	3,310	5.3	40,942
16 to 24 years............	16,772	9,676	57.7	8,587	51.2	1,089	11.3	7,096
25 to 34 years............	16,305	12,790	78.4	12,104	74.2	686	5.4	3,515
35 to 44 years............	17,099	13,335	78.0	12,758	74.6	577	4.3	3,765
45 to 54 years............	19,187	14,758	76.9	14,223	74.1	535	3.6	4,429
55 to 64 years............	15,172	9,050	59.7	8,725	57.5	325	3.6	6,122
65 years and over... ...	18,511	2,495	13.5	2,397	13.0	98	3.9	16,016
Foreign born[2]								
16 years and over........	17,629	9,663	54.8	9,082	51.5	581	6.0	7,966
16 to 24 years............	1,803	819	45.4	734	40.7	85	10.4	984
25 to 34 years............	3,689	2,240	60.7	2,096	56.8	145	6.5	1,449
35 to 44 years............	4,033	2,755	68.3	2,602	64.5	153	5.6	1,278
45 to 54 years............	3,260	2,317	71.1	2,183	67.0	134	5.8	943
55 to 64 years............	2,195	1,220	55.6	1,168	53.2	52	4.3	975
65 years and over... ...	2,648	312	11.8	300	11.3	13	4.0	2,336

See footnotes at end of table.

Table 37. Employment status of the native-born and foreign-born civilian noninstitutional population by age and sex, 2008 annual averages—Continued

(Numbers in thousands)

Country of birth, age, and sex	Civilian noninsti-tutional population	Civilian labor force							Not in labor force
		Total	Percent of population	Employed		Unemployed			
				Total	Percent of population	Total	Percent of labor force		
Men									
Native born[1]									
16 years and over........	95,424	68,119	71.4	63,908	67.0	4,211	6.2		27,305
16 to 24 years............	16,867	10,145	60.1	8,635	51.2	1,510	14.9		6,722
25 to 34 years............	15,696	14,306	91.1	13,413	85.5	893	6.2		1,390
35 to 44 years............	16,273	14,913	91.6	14,226	87.4	687	4.6		1,360
45 to 54 years............	18,170	15,864	87.3	15,223	83.8	641	4.0		2,305
55 to 64 years............	14,192	9,865	69.5	9,507	67.0	357	3.6		4,328
65 years and over......	14,226	3,027	21.3	2,903	20.4	123	4.1		11,199
Foreign born [2]									
16 years and over........	17,688	14,400	81.4	13,578	76.8	822	5.7		3,288
16 to 24 years............	2,042	1,392	68.2	1,245	61.0	147	10.5		650
25 to 34 years............	4,303	3,996	92.9	3,770	87.6	226	5.7		307
35 to 44 years............	4,294	4,059	94.5	3,872	90.2	188	4.6		235
45 to 54 years............	3,342	3,063	91.7	2,901	86.8	163	5.3		279
55 to 64 years............	1,931	1,480	76.6	1,412	73.1	68	4.6		451
65 years and over......	1,776	409	23.0	379	21.4	30	7.3		1,367

[1] Native-born persons are those who were born in the United States or a U.S. Island Area such as Puerto Rico, or born abroad of a U.S.-citizen parent.

[2] Foreign born refers to people residing in the United States who were born outside the United States or one of its outlying areas, such as Puerto Rico or Guam, to parents neither of whom was a U.S. citizen. This group includes legally admitted immigrants, refugees, students, temporary workers, and undocumented aliens.

SOURCE: Current Population Survey, U.S. Department of Labor, U.S. Bureau of Labor Statistics.

Table 38. **Union affiliation of employed wage and salary workers by sex, annual averages, 1983-2008**

(Numbers in thousands)

| Year | Total, both sexes | | | | | Women | | | | |
| | Total employed | Members of unions [1] | | Represented by unions [2] | | Total employed | Members of unions [1] | | Represented by unions [2] | |
		Total	Percent of employed	Total	Percent of employed		Total	Percent of employed	Total	Percent of employed
1983.......	88,290	17,717	20.1	20,532	23.3	40,433	5,908	14.6	7,262	18.0
1984.......	92,194	17,340	18.8	19,932	21.6	42,172	5,829	13.8	7,100	16.8
1985.......	94,521	16,996	18.0	19,358	20.5	43,506	5,732	13.2	6,910	15.9
1986 [3].....	96,903	16,975	17.5	19,278	19.9	44,961	5,802	12.9	6,961	15.5
1987.......	99,303	16,913	17.0	19,051	19.2	46,365	5,842	12.6	6,907	14.9
1988.......	101,407	17,002	16.8	19,241	19.0	47,495	5,982	12.6	7,109	15.0
1989.......	103,480	16,960	16.4	19,198	18.6	48,691	6,141	12.6	7,243	14.9
1990 [3].....	104,876	16,776	16.0	19,105	18.2	49,323	6,179	12.5	7,330	14.9
1991.......	103,723	16,612	16.0	18,790	18.1	49,105	6,142	12.5	7,247	14.8
1992.......	104,668	16,418	15.7	18,578	17.7	49,842	6,274	12.6	7,411	14.9
1993.......	106,101	16,627	15.7	18,682	17.6	50,626	6,516	12.9	7,610	15.0
1994 [3].....	107,989	16,748	15.5	18,850	17.5	51,419	6,642	12.9	7,740	15.1
1995.......	110,038	16,360	14.9	18,346	16.7	52,369	6,430	12.3	7,479	14.3
1996.......	111,960	16,269	14.5	18,158	16.2	53,488	6,410	12.0	7,397	13.8
1997 [3].....	114,533	16,110	14.1	17,923	15.6	54,708	6,347	11.6	7,304	13.4
1998 [3].....	116,730	16,211	13.9	17,918	15.4	55,757	6,362	11.4	7,280	13.1
1999 [3].....	118,963	16,477	13.9	18,182	15.3	57,050	6,528	11.4	7,425	13.0
2000 [3].....	122,089	16,334	13.4	18,153	14.9	58,427	6,671	11.4	7,662	13.1
2001.......	122,229	16,305	13.3	18,026	14.7	58,582	6,768	11.6	7,672	13.1
2002.......	121,826	16,145	13.3	17,695	14.5	58,555	6,820	11.6	7,629	13.0
2003 [3].....	122,358	15,776	12.9	17,448	14.3	59,122	6,732	11.4	7,601	12.9
2004.......	123,554	15,472	12.5	17,087	13.8	59,408	6,593	11.1	7,450	12.5
2005......	125,889	15,685	12.5	17,223	13.7	60,423	6,815	11.3	7,626	12.6
2006......	128,237	15,359	12.0	16,860	13.1	61,426	6,702	10.9	7,501	12.2
2007.......	129,767	15,670	12.1	17,243	13.3	62,299	6,903	11.1	7,749	12.4
2008 [3].....	129,377	16,098	12.4	17,761	13.7	62,532	7,160	11.4	8,036	12.9

See footnotes at end of table.

Table 38. **Union affiliation of employed wage and salary workers by sex, annual averages, 1983-2008—Continued**

(Numbers in thousands)

Year	Men				
	Total employed	Members of unions [1]		Represented by unions [2]	
		Total	Percent of employed	Total	Percent of employed
1983.......	47,856	11,809	24.7	13,270	27.7
1984.......	50,022	11,511	23.0	12,832	25.7
1985.......	51,015	11,264	22.1	12,448	24.4
1986 [3].....	51,942	11,173	21.5	12,317	23.7
1987.......	52,938	11,071	20.9	12,144	22.9
1988.......	53,912	11,019	20.4	12,132	22.5
1989.......	54,789	10,820	19.7	11,955	21.8
1990 [3]....	55,553	10,597	19.1	11,775	21.2
1991.......	54,618	10,470	19.2	11,542	21.1
1992.......	54,826	10,144	18.5	11,167	20.4
1993.......	55,475	10,112	18.2	11,072	20.0
1994 [3]....	56,570	10,106	17.9	11,110	19.6
1995.......	57,669	9,929	17.2	10,868	18.8
1996.......	58,473	9,859	16.9	10,761	18.4
1997 [3]....	59,825	9,763	16.3	10,619	17.7
1998 [3]....	60,973	9,850	16.2	10,638	17.4
1999 [3]....	61,914	9,949	16.1	10,758	17.4
2000 [3]....	63,662	9,664	15.2	10,491	16.5
2001.......	63,647	9,538	15.0	10,354	16.3
2002.......	63,272	9,325	14.7	10,066	15.9
2003 [3]....	63,236	9,044	14.3	9,848	15.6
2004.......	64,145	8,878	13.8	9,638	15.0
2005......	65,466	8,870	13.5	9,597	14.7
2006.......	66,811	8,657	13.0	9,360	14.0
2007.......	67,468	8,767	13.0	9,494	14.1
2008 [3]....	66,846	8,938	13.4	9,724	14.5

[1] Data refer to members of a labor union or an employee association similar to a union.

[2] Data refer to workers who are not members of unions but whose jobs are covered by a union or employee association contract, as well as to members of a labor union or an employee association similar to a union.

[3] Not strictly comparable with data for prior years. For an explanation, see the Historical Comparability documentation provided at **http://www.bls.gov/cps/eetech_methods.pdf**.

NOTE: Data refer to the sole or principal job of full- and part-time workers. All self-employed workers are excluded, regardless of whether their businesses are incorporated.

SOURCE: Current Population Survey, U.S. Department of Labor, U.S. Bureau of Labor Statistics.

Technical Note

The estimates in this report were obtained from the Current Population Survey (CPS), a national monthly sample survey of approximately 60,000 households, which provides a wide range of information on the labor force, employment, and unemployment. Earnings and union affiliation data are collected from one-fourth of the CPS monthly sample. The survey is conducted for the U.S. Bureau of Labor Statistics by the U.S. Census Bureau, using a scientifically selected national sample with coverage in all 50 States and the District of Columbia.

Material in this report is in the public domain and may be reproduced without permission. This information is available to sensory-impaired individuals on request. Voice phone: (202) 691-5200; TDD message referral phone number: 1-800-877-8339.

Reliability of the Estimates

Statistics based on the CPS are subject to both sampling and nonsampling error. When a sample, rather than an entire population, is surveyed, there is a chance that the sample estimates may differ from the "true" population values they represent. The exact difference, or *sampling error,* varies depending on the particular sample selected, and this variability is measured by the standard error of the estimate. There is about a 90-percent chance, or level of confidence, that an estimate based on a sample will differ by no more than 1.6 standard errors from the true population value because of sampling error. BLS analyses generally are conducted at the 90-percent level of confidence.

All other types of error are referred to as *nonsampling error.* Nonsampling error can occur for many reasons, including the failure to sample a segment of the population, inability to obtain information for all respondents in the sample, inability or unwillingness of respondents to provide correct information, and errors made in the collection or processing of data. CPS data also are affected by nonsampling error. The full extent of nonsampling error is unknown, but special studies have been conducted to quantify some sources of such error in the CPS. For further discussion of the reliability of data from the CPS and information on estimating standard errors, see the Household Data technical documentation provided at **http://www.bls.gov/cps/eetech_methods.pdf**.

Concepts and Definitions

Civilian noninstitutional population. Included are persons 16 years of age and older residing in the 50 States and the District of Columbia who are not confined to institutions (for example, correctional facilities and residential nursing and mental health care facilities), and who are not on active duty in the Armed Forces.

Civilian labor force. This group comprises all persons classified as employed or unemployed.

Employed persons. Employed persons are those who, during the survey week, (a) did any work at all as paid civilians; (b) worked in their own business or profession or on their own farm; (c) worked 15 hours or more as unpaid workers in a family business; or (d) were temporarily absent from their jobs because of illness, vacation, bad weather, or another reason.

Unemployed persons. Unemployed persons are those who had no employment during the survey week, were available for work at that time, and made specific efforts to find employment sometime in the prior 4 weeks. Persons laid off from their former jobs and awaiting recall did not need to be looking for work to be classified as unemployed.

Civilian labor force participation rate. This rate is the civilian labor force as a percent of the civilian noninstitutional population.

Employment-population ratio. This ratio represents the proportion of the population that is employed.

Unemployment rate. This rate represents the number of unemployed persons as a percent of the civilian labor force.

Race. White, black or African American, and Asian are terms used to describe the race of persons. Persons in these categories are those who selected that race group only. Data for the remaining race categories—American Indian or Alaska Native, Native Hawaiian or Other Pacific Islanders, and persons who selected more than one race category—are included in totals but are not shown separately because the number of survey respondents was too small to develop estimates of sufficient quality for publication. In the survey process, race is determined by the household respondent.

Hispanic or Latino ethnicity. This term refers to persons who identified themselves in the survey as being Spanish,

Hispanic, or Latino. Persons whose ethnicity is identified as Hispanic or Latino may be of any race.

Family. A family is a group of two or more persons residing together who are related by birth, marriage, or adoption. Families are classified either as married-couple families or as families maintained by women or men without spouses.

Self-employed workers. Self-employed workers are those who work for profit or fees in their own business, profession, trade, or farm. Unincorporated self-employed are included in the self-employed category. Self-employed persons whose businesses are incorporated are included in wage and salary employment.

Wage and salary workers. These are workers who receive wages, salaries, commissions, tips, payment in kind, or piece rates. The group includes employees in both the private and public sectors but, for purposes of the earnings series, excludes all self-employed persons, both those with incorporated businesses as well as those with unincorporated businesses.

Hourly paid workers. Workers who are paid an hourly wage are a subset of wage and salary workers, representing approximately three-fifths of all wage and salary workers. Workers paid by the hour are included in the estimates of median usual weekly earnings in this report, along with salaried workers and other workers not paid by the hour.

Usual weekly earnings. Data are collected on wages and salaries before taxes and other deductions and include any overtime pay, commissions, or tips usually received (at the principal job in the case of multiple jobholders). Earnings of self-employed workers are excluded, regardless of whether their businesses are incorporated. Prior to 1994, respondents were asked to report earnings per week. Since January 1994, respondents have been asked to identify the easiest way for them to report earnings (hourly, weekly, biweekly, twice monthly, monthly, annually, or other) and how much they usually earn in the reported period. Earnings reported on a basis other than weekly are converted to a weekly equivalent. The term "usual" is as perceived by the respondent. If the respondent asks for a definition of usual, interviewers are instructed to define the term as "more than half the weeks worked during the past 4 or 5 months."

Medians of weekly earnings. The median is the amount that divides a given earnings distribution into two equal groups, one having earnings above the median, and the other having earnings below the median. The BLS estimating procedure for determining the median of an earnings distribution places each reported or calculated weekly earnings value into a $50-wide interval that is centered on a multiple of $50. The value of the median is estimated through a linear interpolation of the interval in which the median lies. Over-the-year changes in the medians for specific groups may not

necessarily be consistent with the movements estimated for the overall group boundary. The most common reasons for this possible anomaly follow: (1) There could be a change in the relative weights of the subgroups. For example, the medians of both 16- to 24-year-olds and those 25 years and over may rise, but if the lower earning 16-to-24 age group accounts for a greatly increased share of the total, the overall median could actually fall. (2) There could be a large change in the shape of the distribution of reported earnings. This could be caused by survey observations that are clustered at rounded values, for example, $300, $400, or $500. An estimate lying in a $50-wide centered interval containing such a cluster, or "spike," tends to change more slowly than one in other intervals. For example, medians measure the central tendency of a multipeaked distribution that shifts over time. As the distribution shifts, the median does not necessarily move at the same rate. Specifically, the median takes relatively more time to move through a frequently reported interval, but, once above the upper limit of such an interval, it can move relatively quickly to the next frequently reported earnings interval. BLS procedures for estimating medians mitigate such irregular movements of the measures; however, users should be cautious of these effects when evaluating short-term changes in the medians, as well as in ratios of the medians.

Hours at work. These are the actual hours worked (at all jobs) during the reference week. For example, persons who normally work 40 hours a week but were off during the Columbus Day holiday would be reported as working 32 hours, even though they were paid for the holiday.

Usual hours, or *usual full- or part-time status.* Data on persons "at work" exclude persons who were temporarily absent from a job and therefore classified in the zero-hours worked category, "with a job but not at work." These are persons who were absent from their jobs for the entire week for reasons such as bad weather, vacation, illness, or involvement in a labor dispute. To differentiate a person's normal schedule from his or her activity during the reference week, persons also are classified according to their usual full- or part-time status. In this context, *full-time workers* are those who usually worked 35 hours or more (at all jobs combined). This group includes some individuals who worked less than 35 hours in the reference week for either economic or noneconomic reasons and those who were temporarily absent from work. Similarly, *part-time workers* are those who usually work less than 35 hours per week (at all jobs), regardless of the number of hours worked in the reference week. This may include some individuals who worked more than 34 hours in the reference week, as well as those who were temporarily absent from work.

Occupation and industry. This information applies to the job held during the reference week. Persons with two or more jobs are classified in the occupation and industry at which they worked the greatest number of hours. The occupational and industry classification of CPS data is based on the 2002 Census Bureau occupational and industrial classification systems, which are derived from the 2000 Standard Occupation Classification (SOC) and the 2002 North American Industry Classification System (NAICS). Additional information about these classifications is available online at **http://www. bls.gov/cps/cpsoccind.htm**.

Work experience. These data reflect work activity during the calendar year and are obtained from the Annual Social and Economic Supplement (ASEC) to the Current Population Survey. Estimates of *persons who worked* were based on "yes" responses to the following questions in the ASEC: "Did you work at a job or business at any time during [the survey reference year]?" or "Did you do any temporary, part-time, or seasonal work even for a few days during [the survey reference year]?" Since the reference period is a full year, the number of persons with some employment or un-

employment greatly exceeds the average levels for any given month, which are based on a 1-week reference period, and the corresponding annual averages of monthly estimates.

Poverty classification. Poverty statistics presented in this report are based on definitions developed by the Social Security Administration in 1964 and revised by the Federal interagency committees in 1969 and 1981. These definitions originally were based on the Department of Agriculture's Economy Food Plan and reflected the different consumption requirements of families, based on factors such as family size and the number of children under 18 years of age. The actual poverty thresholds vary in accordance with the makeup of the family. Poverty thresholds are updated each year to reflect changes in the Consumer Price Index for All Urban Consumers (CPI-U). The thresholds do not vary geographically. For more information on poverty data and thresholds, see **http://www.census.gov/hhes/www/poverty/poverty. html**.